Get Ready to Read!

Other Redleaf Guides for Parents

- *Behavior Matters*
- *Not Just a Babysitter*

Get Ready to Read!
Making Child Care Work for You

Sally Moomaw and Brenda Hieronymus
with Yvonne Pearson

Redleaf Press
www.redleafpress.org

Published by Redleaf Press
a division of Resources for Child Caring
10 Yorkton Court
St. Paul, MN 55117
Visit us online at www.redleafpress.org.

The poems on pages 34, 37, 39, 40, 55, and 59 are from *More Than Letters* by
Sally Moomaw and Brenda Hieronymus.

First edition 2006
Cover illustration by Patrice Barton
Interior typeset in Adobe Caslon
Interior illustrations by Chris Wold Dyrud
Printed in the United States of America
13 12 11 10 09 08 07 06   1 2 3 4 5 6 7 8

Redleaf Press books are available at a special discount when purchased in bulk
for special premiums and sales promotions. For details, contact the sales man-
ager at 800-423-8309.

Library of Congress Cataloging-in-Publication Data

Moomaw, Sally, 1948–
  Get ready to read! : making child care work for you / Sally Moomaw and
Brenda Hieronymus with Yvonne Pearson.— 1st ed.
      p. cm.
  ISBN-13: 978-1-929610-74-7
  ISBN-10: 1-929610-74-2
1. Reading (Early childhood)—United States. 2. Language arts (Early child-
hood)—United States. 3. Early childhood education—Activity programs—
United States. I. Hieronymus, Brenda, 1945– II. Pearson, Yvonne. III. Title.
  LB1139.5.R43M66 2006
  372.41—dc22
                                          2006001091

Printed on acid-free paper.

Get Ready to Read!

Introduction

We all want our children to grow up smart and competent, able to take care of themselves in an increasingly complex world, a world that demands literacy. And learning to read and write begins with learning to talk and to listen.

The good news is that babies arrive programmed to develop language skills. If brains were soil, then babies' brains would be the richest black dirt you could find. And the brains of young children are ripe for learning language. The neural pathways necessary for acquiring language skills form at an incredible rate, so early childhood is a fertile time for sowing the seeds of literacy.

For children, play is both how they have fun and how they explore and learn about themselves and the world. It's through play that children learn how to learn, and that includes learning language skills and eventually learning to read and write. That's why, at child care homes and centers and at preschools, what the children do all day appears to be simply organized play, rather than structured learning. In the most effective settings and programs, though, the learning is so embedded in play that it doesn't feel like work to children.

While playing with each other, children get a lot of practice in using their language skills (talking and listening) and earliest literacy skills (reading and writing). Whether your child is at home or is in a family child care setting, a child care center, or a preschool, if she's regularly and actively engaged in conversation with caring, attentive adults and other children and is encouraged to creatively interact with an environment rich with oral and written language, she's already learning to learn how to read and write. As a parent, you can do much to support and collaborate with your provider in consciously creating a rich experience for your child. By building on what your child is learning at child care or preschool and by letting the provider or teacher know what your child is learning at home, you can become a partner with your child care provider or teacher in supporting your child's language and literacy development.

Children Learn by Playing

Remember, language-rich play experiences provide the context that helps young children make the transition from language development to reading and writing. For young children to eventually care about reading and writing, written words have to make sense, they have to have meaning. When children see and use words in the course of play activities that have meaning, those words take on meaning in the context of that activity. This key principle led to the development of structured play activities and play environments in child care and preschool settings. These activities and environments *are* the curriculum and they almost always include developmentally appropriate language and literacy components.

This book offers information on how children learn to

read and write so you can effectively collaborate with your preschool teacher or child care provider to encourage your child's literacy skills.

Understanding how children develop literacy skills is also valuable in helping you recognize when and how your child is learning as he plays at home. After all, a child's process of learning literacy skills is not visible in the way that learning a physical skill is. It's clear, for example, that it doesn't make sense to encourage a child to walk if he can't yet sit up. Only once you've seen your child trying to take steps do you encourage him in learning to walk. The process of learning literacy skills is not so obvious. To help make the development of literacy skills more concrete, we've included a number of developmentally appropriate (i.e., designed to match a typical preschooler's learning abilities), fun, and easy games and activities that have proven effective in supporting the development of those skills.

Understanding how children learn can also help you recognize whether a preschool or child care center uses appropriate methods to prepare young children for kindergarten and beyond. Testing has become a pronounced part of the educational environment, and some elementary schools and even preschools teach lessons specifically to help children pass a test. This generally unhelpful practice is especially so in preschool. Preschools or child care centers may drill children over and over again in phonemes—the discrete sounds that make up a word. They may emphasize learning one letter per week, one at a time, isolated from a letter's meaning within a word or situation. They may use worksheets, such as tracing letters, to teach writing. But, because their brains aren't ready to process information on this level, this kind of teaching is generally a waste of time for preschool children.

The alphabet is an abstraction. In other words, the letters of the alphabet are symbols representing the idea of sounds. The brains of children who are three to five years old are developmentally incapable of understanding abstract information. Memorizing a string of letters makes no sense to them. Although they may be able to parrot the information, they won't be able to understand it or use it as a foundation for more learning.

Even worse than the wasted time is the likelihood that a child will end up experiencing learning to read and write as drudgery and too difficult and will be turned off at an early age. What matters is that young children enjoy learning how to learn, which is what happens naturally in the course of play, whether it's structured or spontaneous. Likewise, if children are read to from an early age, if they have fun with books, they'll want to read. And if they enjoy reading, they're likely to read more, which is the best way to learn to read better. If children develop these skills naturally at their own pace, they're more likely to be ready for the formal instruction in reading and writing they'll encounter in primary school. Consequently, they'll be able to acquire the skills and knowledge that testing measures.

Increasing use of content standards is directly related

to the growing use of testing at earlier ages. Many states have adopted academic content standards—statements of what must be included in a curriculum—for children from preschool through twelfth grade. The federal government has also developed outcome measures for Head Start children. Content standards are an attempt by legislators to ensure that educational programs adequately prepare children at each grade level.

For the most part, educational standards offer appropriate benchmarks for evaluating the progress of young children and the fitness of programs. Be aware, however, that the content in preschool academic standards must be taught in developmentally appropriate ways. Most states recognize this and exert concerted effort on ensuring that preschool programs approach standards through a curriculum that emphasizes use of developmentally appropriate techniques and activities, such as stories, songs, and rhymes, and the thoughtful use of play environments (areas in centers and preschools that are set up for specific kinds of play activities). Parents still need to be vigilant, however, as some policy makers, preschool teachers, and child care providers have succumbed to the pressure to meet rigid standards in ways that don't account for individual differences in development, cultural differences, and variations in children's learning styles.

Partnering with the Teacher or Provider

No matter what kind of setting your child is in, there are many ways you can play an active role in partnering with your provider to help your child as she develops language and literacy skills. Preschools generally have a curriculum that includes early reading and writing activities. Child care centers and family child care settings can vary from having an informal story time and some books available for reading to having a highly developed literacy curriculum. This is why it's important to schedule some time with your provider to find out specifically what she is doing to foster language and literacy development for the children in her care.

This book offers ideas for supporting your child's activities in whatever kind of setting she's in, ideas for enhancing her activities, and ideas for initiating activities.

Chapter 1 presents information from recent research on how children learn to read and write. Chapters 2 through 5 look specifically at reading and offer a number of play activities that give children an opportunity to enhance their early reading skills. Chapters 6 through 9 focus on play activities that support emerging writing skills, and chapter 10 focuses on games that help build a foundation for both reading and writing. The activities presented in these chapters are similar to those offered in preschools and some child care centers and can be adapted to other settings as well, including your home and family child care. If your child's care setting is a nonstructured one, you can offer these activities as tools to enhance your child's experience when he's there.

It's easy and fun to support your child's natural drive to learn how to read and write. We hope this book will help you expand your repertoire, feel confident as your child's helpmate and guide, and—most of all—have fun with your child.

Chapter 1
How Children Learn to Read and Write

Julia was almost two years old. One night as her mother was putting her to bed, Julia looked up at her and asked, "Babo?" Knowing what Julia wanted, her mother said, "Let's ask daddy to bring up your bottle." But before her mother could call downstairs to her father, Julia yelled at the top of her lungs, "Daddy, a da do toi babo!"

Although what she said made her mother and father burst out laughing, Julia was doing serious work. She was demonstrating her emerging understanding of language. She had just placed her word for bottle in the position of object in a full sentence, though the other "words" in her sentence were simply placeholders.

Julia was figuring out how to use verbs as well. When her parents wanted to encourage her to eat, they'd say "Mmmm" as they offered her food. Her mother would hand her a bit of banana and say, "Mmmm." Or her dad would eat a spoonful of squash and say, "Mmmm." When they read Maurice Sendak's *In the Night Kitchen* with Julia, every time they came to the page where the cook is stirring batter in a bowl, Julia would say, "Mmmm." Her parents assumed she meant that the food looked good. But one day when Julia's dad was cooking fish she said, "Daddy mmmm." It was then they realized she'd used her first verb.

How Children Develop an Understanding of Language

As dear and funny as they are, children's early attempts at language teach us that children learn to read and write in much the same way they learn to talk. A lot of research has been conducted on how children learn language and literacy skills, and many preschools and child care centers use this research to support the learning efforts of the children in their care. In this chapter, we share with you what some of this research says about how children accomplish this learning so it will be easier for you to partner with your child's provider or teacher. We encourage you to ask questions and find out how—or if—the teacher or provider uses this information in her work with your child.

Children begin thinking very early on, trying to make sense of their world. Learning seems to be driven by a search for coherence, for logical connections. Children develop ideas from observing other people and then they test their ideas. They construct rules for themselves and then refine those rules to fit with their experiences. They explore their ideas and collect evidence that either supports their ideas or requires them to change their ideas.

Of course, since children cannot think abstractly, they

don't say to themselves, "I'm going to see if this rule I've constructed about verbs is accurate." Nevertheless, we adults can see that this is what they're doing. And the best thing we can do to help them learn is to encourage them to keep forming and testing their ideas.

>How Children Learn to Talk

Knowing that children learn to read and write in much the same way they learn to talk, we can figure out how best to help them with early reading and writing by looking at the way they learn to talk—and the ways they *don't* learn to talk. No one sits down with a child and says, "Today we're going to have a lesson on talking. Verbs come after subjects. 'Dog' is an example of a subject and 'runs' is an example of a verb.'" Nor does anyone say to a child, "You form plurals by adding an 's' to the word, but there are some exceptions. 'Bear' becomes 'bears,' but 'deer' is the same in its singular and plural forms."

Instead, you talk to your child, and you notice the sounds he's making and the words he's saying, and you converse with him. If your child says, "Look at the deers," you reply with something such as, "Aren't the deer pretty?" You know your child is developing an understanding of plurals, because he added an "s" to "deer." You do not correct the mistake; instead, you model back for your child. Your response lets him learn by experience that there are exceptions.

Interestingly, children follow the same developmental steps in all languages. For instance, when babies are about six months old they generally begin to imitate sounds from the specific language they hear spoken. So babies in Spanish-speaking countries will trill the *r* sound, and babies in a German-speaking country will practice guttural sounds. But babies learning English won't make either of these sounds.

When children begin to use words in combinations, they use them according to the grammatical rules of the language they're learning. Children learning English will put the subject before the verb, and later, the object after the verb. They will construct rules and overgeneralize from those rules. So if "ear" becomes "ears," "child" will become "childs." And then they figure out the exceptions.

As in learning to talk, your child learns what written words mean by the context in which they're used. Both when learning to talk and when learning to read and write, children get the whole meaning, and then they learn how the parts contribute to the whole. So the teaching for these skills should be similar.

Teaching Literacy Skills

In the past, formal teaching of reading and writing began in the first grade, by first teaching children the names of the alphabet letters, then how to write them, and then how to put them together in simple words. Schools taught reading by breaking down words into sounds, or phonemes, assuming that children could put the phonemes together to read the whole word. Research on how young children learn has brought about changes in this approach to teaching, particularly for preschool children.

What educators came to realize was that children actually begin the process of learning to read and write as early as infancy. When, for example, you read board books to your baby and she notices that there are markings on a page and that you turn the pages as you read, she's taking her first step into reading. When you've read your toddler a book about a bunny a million times and she starts to say "bunny" as soon as she sees the first picture, she's taking another step into reading. As soon as she makes her first purposeful line with a crayon, she's taking her first step into writing. By the time she's three or four years old, she may be carefully constructing a circle or even pretending to scribble sentences. If she's an older preschooler, she may even be recognizing certain letters or special words.

Although preschoolers are learning the skills required for reading and writing, this doesn't necessarily mean they're ready to learn to read and write sentences. As we said earlier, the most recent research suggests that children learn through their own experiences and the thinking that these experiences lead to. They develop their own ideas about language—both spoken and written—and then they test these ideas in their play situations and environments.

What you need to do is give your child lots of opportunities to observe and experiment with letters, numbers, shapes, and colors. You can have conversations with your child that encourage him to think about these things and that help him refine his thoughts. This book is filled with ideas for how you can work with a teacher or a provider to offer your child such opportunities and to help him make personal sense of them.

Effective teaching encourages children to think, explore, and experiment. In preschools and in most centers, language concepts, which are part and parcel of children's play, are fostered in an active learning environment through hands-on activities that help children develop observation and analysis skills, make predictions, problem-solve, and experiment. For example, a group of children might play "grocery store" in the dramatic play area of a center, with two or three children as the shoppers and another as the cashier. The children might "write" grocery lists and use labels for the various food sections and items, which they discuss as they make their purchases. During such an activity, children are learning how to learn, an approach that will serve them well from kindergarten to the elementary grades and all the way through college.

> *Educators use several formal concepts when they design the language and literacy parts of their curriculum. Although the terminology may make them sound complicated, the concepts are really very simple, and they tell us something about the process a child naturally goes through as he or she learns about language.*

- *Sound-symbol relationships.* This simply means a child can recognize that there is a relationship between a sound and the way it looks on the page. In educational jargon, the distinct unit of a word that makes its own sound is called a phoneme.

- *Voice-print pairing.* This means a child can pair each spoken word with its written counterpart.
- *Boundaries of words.* This refers to a child recognizing that words have a beginning and an end and that there is space between two words.
- *Left-to-right and top-to-bottom text progression.* Children notice that there is a certain direction to reading, which, of course, may vary depending on their native language. In this book, we are talking about learning English.
- *Use of upper- and lowercase letters.*

A Balanced Approach

Many preschools and elementary schools have adopted a balanced approach to teaching reading and writing. This can involve a mix of working with children on phonics and phonemic awareness, helping them to read meaningful literature when they are ready, and creating language-rich environments where learning is built into a child's everyday play and exploration. So an important feature of a balanced approach to teaching is that the concepts of reading and writing are taught in every aspect of a preschool's curriculum and in all aspects of a child care day. For instance, when Keisha was having trouble letting her mom leave in the mornings, the preschool teacher helped Keisha write a note to her mother. Keisha appeared to be more comfortable after this and soon stopped protesting when it was time for her mother to leave. When Carlo ran ahead of the other children toward the intersection, the child care provider asked him to wait. She then pointed out the stop sign at the end of the street, and read it to him. Besides taking very practical steps to care for the children, this teacher and this provider were also teaching literacy skills.

With a balanced approach, the teacher or provider constantly looks for opportunities to encourage reading and writing. She includes toy traffic signs with building blocks, points out words on food containers or Band-Aid boxes, and asks children to help label their own artwork. Children are asked questions about words and encouraged to think about them. In this kind of teaching, children are provided with environments and situations in which they can do a lot of discovering for themselves. The teacher or provider becomes a facilitator of each child's natural curiosity and drive to learn.

As a parent, you can play this same role with your child. You can engage your child in pleasant and interesting conversations. You can read to your child regularly. You can talk about the pictures in a book and ask your child questions about the story. Should you point out the letters and sounds as you read to her? Sometimes—when your child seems interested in that. Should you correct the spelling error when your child writes "cudn't" instead of "couldn't"? Maybe not—it depends on your child's interest and the situation.

You may fear that encouraging literacy skills in your preschooler demands more knowledge and skill than you have. Don't worry. Gaining knowledge may be a useful and interesting backdrop, but teaching your child is really about encouraging his exploration as he plays, giving him lots of affirmation, and tuning in. If you ask your child what sound the "c" in "cool" makes and he totally ignores you, he's not ready. Don't push it. Learning should never be a burden to a young child—let him have fun in his play. And you, too, should have fun sharing his learning experiences.

Developmental Steps in Learning Literacy Skills

As children explore books they begin to understand that the print on the page means something. They know that a blank page of white paper is different from a page of paper with words printed on it, and that pictures are different from print. English-speaking children observe that people read from the top to the bottom of a page and from left to right.

Later (usually around age four or five), children understand that there are individual words in the stream of writing. Not until they know that print has meaning and that print is broken down into words do they realize that words are made up of individual letters. Finally, they look at the parts of words and make connections between sounds and letters.

Children learn in exactly the opposite way many adults think they learned how to read. Instead of constructing, children deconstruct, rather like taking apart a clock and putting it back together to see how it works. They go not from learning the alphabet to learning words and then on to sentences and paragraphs to pages, but in the opposite direction.

Children also progress through predictable stages as

they learn to write. (See pages 76–80 for a full description of these stages.) These stages are similar to those they go through when they learn to talk, and this appears to be true regardless of which language a child is learning. As is true with talking, young children form and test ideas about writing as they experiment with making marks on paper. In other words, they try to make personal sense of writing.

Understanding how children learn to talk, to read, and to write can help prepare you to talk about your child's education with your care provider or teacher. It can help you recognize the ways in which you are already teaching your child language and literacy skills during the normal course of the day, so you can use those opportunities even more effectively. It can also help you partner with your child care provider in supporting your child's learning, which can promote a synergy between home and child care.

Being a Partner with the Provider or Teacher

The best thing you and your child's provider or preschool teacher can do to help your child learn to read and write is to provide models of rich language and provide her with lots of opportunities to observe and experiment. Give her lots of experiences with books that fit her level of language and understanding and that will interest her. Offer her crayons and pencils and paper. Point out signs and read them out loud to her. Let her see you reading magazines and writing shopping lists.

You can begin reading to your child when he's still a

baby. Very young children can handle board books without destroying them. Although he may try to eat the pages, what he'll learn is the idea of a book. You turn pages, you say out loud the words that are associated with pictures, and he starts to form the idea that this thing with pages has meaning. He learns to value reading by watching you read or by watching older siblings read. As time goes on, he learns that there are messages in books and books are fun. He'll associate books and magazines and reading with good feelings.

There are many ways to encourage your child at home and to build on the teaching that occurs in child care during his early years. These can be as simple as giving your child encouragement, asking questions, answering questions, thinking out loud, and suggesting and commenting. You can talk with your child about the books he's "reading" in preschool and child care, share books back and forth between home and school, send notes for your provider to read to your child, and read aloud what your child brings home from child care. Remember that by reading stories, drawing attention to words and letters in a room, engaging in conversations, retelling stories, incorporating written words in play, you already are teaching your child to read and write.

It's also important that teachers, providers, and parents celebrate a child's efforts at reading and writing and avoid any form of correction or criticism. Remember that when Julia said "babo," her mother didn't say, "No, Julia, the word is bottle." Similarly, when Julia is older (usually around three-and-a-half to four years old) and her first attempt at writing her name is "Jla," her teacher or child care provider should share Julia's excitement, not point out that she's spelled her name wrong.

Remember also that each child has his own timing. For instance, some children pick up the idea that words are made of sounds, or phonemes, quickly and easily. Other children need more help to recognize this. In any group of children, there are as many rates of learning as there are children in the group. So, if a child your son's age has mastered the letters of the alphabet but your child has not, you don't need to worry. All children go through the same basic steps in the same order, but they do it at different paces. Your child will get there in his own time. What's important is that you and your child's teacher or provider closely observe your child and support her individual efforts. Then, at parent conferences or in brief updates at drop-off or pick-up times, you can discuss where your child is in her current language and literacy development and coordinate your activities at child care and home accordingly. Following such a plan also allows you to identify early on any behaviors that signal potential developmental issues that may require professional assessment.

Literacy Goals for Very Young Children

Specific literacy goals should be part of any preschool curriculum. Such goals should make it clear that preschoolers are learning only the beginning stages of reading and writing. Depending on how structured the curriculum is in your child care setting, literacy goals may not be stated overtly. Nevertheless, you can use the list of goals that follows as a guideline when you think about how language arts are included in your child's day, whether that day is spent in a preschool, a child care center, or a family child care. Although some of the terms may sound academic, remember that the ideas are simple and that we'll be looking more closely at them as we go through the reading and writing activities in this book.

The literacy goals that should be part of a preschool curriculum (or a preschooler's life) are as follows:

- Developing children's familiarity with and enjoyment of books and reading
- Providing many opportunities for children to interact with print (for instance, through charts and signs and labels along with books and magazines)
- Fostering the construction of letter-sound relationships and letter-word relationships within a meaningful context (for instance, giving children chances during their play to notice that the letter "d" is associated with a certain sound, or that "dog" begins with the letter "d")
- Enhancing vocabulary development ("Are you cold? I'm chilly too.")
- Supporting children's construction of literacy concepts, such as the relationship between spoken and written words (for instance, pointing to the word "dog" when you read it in a book)
- Facilitating reading and writing across the curriculum (encouraging the learning as part of all different aspects of a child's play)

- Expanding children's understanding of book language (that stories have beginnings, middles, and ends)
- Encouraging children's feelings of competency in reading and writing ("You drew the letter 'd.' You're learning to write!")

This book includes specific ideas for encouraging reading and writing and for supporting your child's teacher or care provider's efforts. Children, of course, work on reading and writing and talking all at the same time, so teaching reading and writing separately is impossible. Only for the purposes of a book such as this one can we separate the discussion of how to encourage reading and writing.

Chapter 2
Early Reading

Think how good it can feel at the end of the day to sit quietly with your child, her soft hands near yours, her warm body folded into your lap, as you read aloud a favorite book with its familiar silly or soothing sounds and colorful pictures. Many young children look forward to bedtime stories. And as a parent you probably look forward to them as well—at least on the nights when you're not overwhelmed with a million tasks yet to be done.

This pleasurable activity is also one of the best teaching tools in existence. Reading to your child is a strong motivator for his own reading. From it he learns to associate positive feelings with books, to know that reading is both fun and relaxing, and that it can bring him closer to people. Children want to be like their parents, so if you love reading, you child is apt to as well. He'll want to find out more about what he sees in the books you read together, like the name of that dinosaur with the big spikes down its tail.

As you read regularly to your child, she'll absorb information about the process of reading, information she can eventually use to make sense of how to read herself. For instance, she'll begin to understand that books contain stories, and stories have beginnings, middles, and ends. She'll begin to notice that (with English) you turn the pages from front to back and you read from left to right and top to bottom. She'll even begin to notice that the print on the page is connected to the words you say. And this is the critical point: Print has meaning!

Before children can begin to read, they must first understand that the marks on a piece of paper—letters and words—have meaning. You can expand this sense of meaning by pointing at words that are important to your child as you read them, or pointing out that a word represents an image. "See the boy with the red hat? Here is the word for hat." You can also emphasize the importance of books and reading by using them in your daily life with your child. You can notice aloud that a book in the kitchen tells you how to cook tonight's soup, or that a book is where you find the telephone number for your child's friend.

You can also help your child understand that printed words have meaning by reading aloud words in your everyday life that are important to him, words such as "dog food" on the bag of food you pick up for his puppy, or "men" when you take him to the bathroom at a restaurant. You can write down the words he says so he can send a message to grandma and grandpa. You can write his name on his special bookshelf.

Coordinating with Child Care or Preschool

The kinds of things you do at home to interest your

child in reading are the same kinds of things that pre-school teachers and child care providers do. Following are some ways you can partner with your provider in encouraging reading readiness skills.

> Sharing Books

Sharing information about books is the easiest and simplest way to work with your provider in supporting your child's efforts and excitement about reading. You might, for instance, find out what books are being read at the child care center and borrow one to read again at home, or, if it's a book your child particularly loves, buy it for your home. Or you might lend one of your child's favorite books to your child care provider.

You can also talk with your child's preschool teacher or care provider about the kinds of books that are being read at school and supplement them at home. In preschools, teachers often select a variety of books to extend children's learning opportunities, and you can choose a similar range of books for reading at home.

Predictable books are particularly wonderful for young children. Such books have a repeating text or some other element that creates a predictable pattern. One example is the popular *Goodnight Moon* by Margaret Wise Brown, in which the reader says goodnight repeatedly to objects inside and outside a bedroom. Another popular example is the song "Old MacDonald Had a Farm," with its refrain, "E-I-E-I-O." Predictable books make it easy for children to memorize the words and anticipate what comes next. Not only do children become excited by such a book and attached to it, but, as they say the words along with the adult, it also helps them feel that they, too, are readers.

Preschools and child care centers often have what are called big books. The large pages of these books have print that is easy to read, so a teacher or provider can hold the book up for a group of children to read together. We'll talk more about big books in the next chapter.

>Making Reading a Part of Everyday Activities

Preschools and child care settings build reading into children's play and normal activities throughout the day. Listed below are some additional tools and activities that teachers and child care providers use to encourage children to read. You can use this as a reference when you talk with your provider about the literacy activities available for your child. As we take a closer look at writing, you'll notice that many of these tools and techniques are used to encourage writing as well.

- *Environmental print.* Children are asked to notice printed words around them that are useful to them, from signs and cereal boxes and other real items with print in the neighborhood and play areas, to the large print on such things as name tags, labels, and message boards.

- *Story props.* Props can be used to extend a child's interest in the books she or he loves. Children love to play with familiar items such as the stuffed animals or toy trucks that appear in a favorite book. As they act out a book's story, they practice following the sequence of the story, once again getting the idea that words have meaning. At the same time, they are practicing new vocabulary words.

- *Interactive charts.* Preschool and child care settings often use charts with movable words, such as attendance charts, song charts, or sentence completion games.

- *Word banks.* These collections of cards, each with a different word, let children see in print words that are interesting to them. The words used on cards usually are related to the stories, environmental print, and themes that arise during daily activities in the play areas that make up the preschool's or center's early childhood curriculum.

- *Project documentation.* Such items as journals, scrapbooks, and labeled photo albums allow children to see their thoughts and words in writing. Such documents also record each child's projects and learning progress.

- *Dictation.* Children can begin to understand the relationship between spoken and written language when an adult writes down their stories or ideas exactly as they express them.

- *Manipulative games.* Children move around magnets, blocks, or other objects with letters or words on them to form patterns or words.

- *Group games.* Children share information or do wordplay and develop language skills within a game context.

- *Transition songs.* Short, easy rhyming songs led by the provider or teacher guide children through transitions such as moving from activity to activity, at meal, snack, or nap time, and for arriving or departing. Through repetition and a direct relationship of words to specific behaviors and environments, a child's vocabulary and understanding of how language works expands.

In the following chapters, we'll take a closer look at some of the literacy activities reflected in the preceding list that are typical of those used in preschools and some child care centers. You can collaborate with your child's teacher or provider to extend your child's opportunities for learning from these activities. You also can design and use activities such as the ones presented in this book at home.

Chapter 3
Big Book Activities

Big books are popular items in many preschools and child care centers. They are simply oversized versions of books, containing stories, poems, or songs. Some are nonfiction and feature colorful photographs or drawings. Because the pages are supersized and the print is large, young children can easily see the words as the teacher or provider reads.

The stories, poems, or songs in big books often are repetitive and predictable ones. Big books will have a line of text that gets repeated on several pages with only one or two words changing on each successive page. You can capitalize on the learning your child does by using big books at home or by partnering with your provider to bring big books into the classroom or center.

How Big Books Help Children Learn

Reading big books with young children helps them learn the basic foundational skills of reading and writing. Big books help children understand that the spoken word and the written word are related.

Big books also help young children develop phonemic

awareness. Specifically, the large print makes it easier for children to recognize, discriminate, match, and compare letters and words. It makes it easier for them to see where one word stops and another begins. This, in turn, makes it easier for children to associate a spoken word with the same word in print.

Big books provide yet another chance for children to observe that English writing goes from left to right and top to bottom, to recognize that letters have a function in forming words, and to make sound-letter associations. Older children may begin to discriminate between upper- and lowercase letters and recognize some words. Once they reach this point, children begin the transition from being emergent readers to becoming conventional independent readers.

Big books that are repetitive can help children learn vocabulary and remember sentence construction. This is especially useful if your child has a language delay or is learning English as a second language.

How to Be a Partner with the Provider or Teacher in Using Big Books

One way you can collaborate with your child's teacher or provider in using big books is to find out which ones she's using at school. You can then buy the regular versions for your home library or borrow them from the public library. Or you could ask the provider if you can take a big book home from the center overnight to read with your child.

You could also simply ask your child about the big

book he's using at preschool or at his child care center, or you could let him play with magnetic letters at home and help him make important words from that book. You could also draw with your child pictures related to big books. If the big book is about a certain character your child loves, you might see if you can buy a character doll or stuffed animal that matches it. Or, using a regular version of the book as a guide, you can draw or paint that character and hang the picture in your child's bedroom.

If your child's teacher or provider is not currently using big books, you might find a time when it's convenient for her to talk with you—not, of course, when she's solely responsible for a roomful of children—and discuss the idea with her. Perhaps she doesn't know about this teaching tool. Or she may know about big books but has decided not to use them in her setting. Or perhaps she simply hasn't had time to develop a plan for using them.

That last reason was the case in the family child care that Molly attended. Her mother, Virginia, had a friend whose child was at a Head Start center where big books were used regularly, and Virginia thought Molly would love them. She decided she would talk with Molly's provider, Marion. When Marion said she'd seen the big books and would love to use them, Virginia offered to make one.

Virginia chose one of Molly's favorite books, *Goodnight Moon,* and gathered the large sheets of paper, markers, and pictures she needed to make a big book. First she traced and colored some pictures from *Goodnight Moon* and cut them out. Then she had Molly help her glue a picture of the "old lady" and the moon on the first page of the big book, where she wrote, "Goodnight moon." On the second page, she glued a drawing she and Molly had done of the "child" from the book in bed. Under it she wrote, "Goodnight Molly." She made a page like Molly's for each of the other six children in Marion's child care.

Virginia arranged with Marion a time when she could read the book to the children at child care. Molly absolutely glowed when her mother brought in the book, and the other children loved it as much as Molly did. Virginia left the book with Marion, who began to use it with the children periodically. Interestingly, Marion told Virginia that after she and the children had read the book together several times, she noticed the children were beginning to recognize their names in it.

If you have a big book at home, you might ask the teacher or provider if you or your child could bring it to preschool or child care to share with the other children. If you have time, you might even go to the center and read the book with a group of children. Your provider may appreciate the help, and your child will love having you be part of her day in that setting.

Using Big Books at Home

If you decide to use big books at home, it's important that you read the book to your child enough times that he knows and loves the story before you use it for any teaching. Otherwise, your child is likely to become impatient with the interruptions. While you're reading the book the first few times, talk with your child about the story line and ask questions such as "What will the rabbit do next?" or "Has that ever happened to you?" Once he knows the book well and can join you in saying lines as they come up, you can point out rhymes, phonemes, letters, and so on as you read. For example, if your child has read the story with you enough and recognizes a certain word, you can help him with sound-letter association. Children's first sound-letter associations typically are the initial consonants in words. You could point to the word "fish" as you read it, and emphasize the "f" sound. You could then ask your child if he knows other words that begin with this sound. A child often responds particularly well to the letter that his name begins with.

How to Make Big Books

You can buy big books from bookstores, Web sites, and early childhood catalogs, but you can also make your own. In fact, homemade ones are often better than purchased books, because you can control the content and include your child's name and interests.

Big books last longer if you make them with twelve-by-eighteen-inch construction paper and laminate them. You can print directly on construction paper or you can make sentence strips on a computer and glue them onto the paper. If you choose to write out the sentences, be sure your printing is large and clear and resembles print that your child is used to seeing. If you use a computer, choose the "landscape" setting for printing so you can print words sideways on the paper and therefore make them bigger. Select a font that resembles standard print. Arial and Helvetica are two appropriate fonts. You can draw your own illustrations or cut illustrations from books or magazines. Finally, laminate your pages using lamination film from your local office supply store. When you're finished, you can bind your book by punching two holes along the edge of each page and tying pages together with yarn or ribbon or twine. You could also use notebook rings, but, since they tend to tear paper over time, you might want to use the small reinforcement circles available at office supply stores. Some photocopying centers will even bind homemade books for you.

Sample Activities

Described below are some typical big books, along with activities that you or your provider can do with your child.

>Hello, Good-Bye

This activity, which provides an ideal opportunity to explore how people in other cultures say hello and good-bye, allows children to learn and play at the same time. Children are often fascinated by how words look and sound in languages different from their own. Think how often we adults substitute the greetings and good-byes of other languages for our own English terms. We might say "ciao" instead of "hello," or "au revoir" instead of "see you later." Or maybe we'd say "arrivaderci" or "bon voyage" or "hola" or "adios."

In this handmade big book, a poem is repeated and

the words for "hello" and "good-bye" in different languages are substituted for our English words. Here's the poem:

> *I make new friends the more I grow,*
> *Did you ever wonder why*
> *It's much more fun to say "hello"*
> *Than to have to say "good-bye."*

★ Activity Instructions ★

Many centers make a four-page construction paper book for this poem. You can easily make this same book with six twelve-by-eighteen-inch pieces of white construction paper. Two pieces of paper become the front and back covers of the book, and the other four pieces form the four inside pages.

Each of the pages holds one line from the poem. Using large, clearly written letters, print the sentences on colored strips of paper and glue them to the white construction paper. You might want to illustrate the sentences with pictures of children from various cultures that you've cut from calendars or magazines. Then laminate each page.

On the third and fourth pages, create a pocket at the end of the phrase to hold the words for "hello" and "good-bye." Use lamination film to make the pockets, and tape them on with clear packing tape. Then write words for "hello" and "good-bye" in other languages to insert in the pockets when you read the poem.

Here are some words for "hello" and "good-bye" in other languages:

LANGUAGE	WORD FOR HELLO	WORD FOR GOOD-BYE
Filipino	*mabuhay* (*pronounced* mah-boo-HI)	*paalam* (*pronounced* pah-AH-lahm)
Finnish	*hei* (*pronounced* HEY)	*hei*
Indonesian	*selamat datang* (*pronounced* che-lah-mate dha-thang)	*selamat jalan* (*pronounced* che-lah-mate jah-lane)
Spanish	*hola* (*pronounced* OH-lah)	*adios* (*pronounced* ah-dee-OHS)

You could also use the Internet to find words for "hello" and "good-bye" in additional languages.

After you've read the book with your child enough times that she knows what's coming next and can say the sentences with you, you can begin substituting the words for "hello" and "good-bye" in other languages. Start with just one new language. When your child is comfortable and familiar with those new words, you can add another language. Your child will probably enjoy tucking the new word into the pocket before you read it aloud.

Children quickly learn how to say "hello" and "good-bye" in other languages, and they soon become familiar with how the new words look in written form as well. You might ask as you read, "Do you know what language this is written in?" or "Which one of these two words says 'hello'?" You can encourage sound recognition (phonemic awareness) by asking, "What sound does 'hello' start with?" or "Think of another word that starts with the letter 'h.'" If your child is ready for this step, she'll take you up on it. If not, don't push. Wait and try again later.

You can also incorporate other words in different languages. The book *What Is Your Language?* by Debra Leventhal translates the words "yes" and "no" into other languages. Or perhaps you can use "boy" and "girl" or "up" and "down." Then all you'll need to do is come up with new sentences for the words you choose.

Ideas for Partnering with the Teacher or Provider

- Find out if other languages are spoken by children in your child's class and incorporate them into your big book.
- If the center does not have this big book, lend it to your center or take it to class and read it with the children.
- Read books about cultures that speak the languages you've chosen for your big book or about the cultures of children in your child's class. Share these books with the center.

• Take to the center dress-up clothing or other play props that reflect the cultures represented in your big book.

›Baby Book

Young children are fascinated by babies. If a new baby is brought into a room, other children in the room are drawn to her. They want to touch and watch and pat and talk to her. Young children also tend to be interested in their own baby pictures and in stories of themselves as babies. This makes a class baby book ideal for preschoolers.

The book described here can easily be used by a preschool, child care center, or family child care, and it can be adapted or supplemented at home as well.

When used in a classroom or center, this big book contains a page for each child at the center and includes both a baby photo and a current photo. Each page of the book contains these lines:

> *When I was a baby I looked like this,*
> *Guess who it could be!*

Under this verse is a baby photo. Next comes another verse:

> *Now open the door and you can see*

Under the second verse is a flap that, when opened, reveals a current photo of the child. To the right of the photo are the words, "It's me!"

★ Activity Instructions ★

Again, you can use construction paper and large hand-written or computer-generated print to make the book pages. The flap that covers the current photo can be made of plain or laminated construction paper and attached with packing tape after the page itself has been laminated.

You can adapt this book for home by using photos of classmates, friends, cousins or other extended family members, or siblings and parents. If your child is very young, you may choose to use just two words per page: "baby" under the person's baby photo and the person's name under his current photo. As you read through the book, your child will eagerly guess the identity of babies in the photos. Many children often return to the book and read it on their own as well.

Questions you might ask or comments you might make as you read include, "Who do you think this baby is?" "Can you find the word for 'baby' on this page?" "Look at the word 'I.' It's a letter and a word!" If your child has begun to recognize phonemes, you can also ask about words that end with an "ee" sound, and ask what sound the word "baby" begins with. Then ask what letter makes that sound.

Ideas for Partnering with the Teacher or Provider

• Ask permission to photocopy the baby pictures of the other children at the center, and also take current photos, again if the parents will give permission, and use these photos in the big book at home. When you've completed the book, you can lend it to your provider for use in the classroom. One precaution: If your child's class includes adopted children, it would be better not to include classmates in your book, since children who've been adopted sometimes do not have baby photos.

• Put photos of all the children on a poster board and label the photos with their names.

> Emily's [Substitute Your Child's Name for "Emily"] Mail Book

This big book has the same verse on every page, but each successive page has an envelope with the name of a different person. A message is tucked into the envelope for each person. This book will be slightly different if it is created for your home rather than for use at preschool or child care. For example, at home the book may say

Emily's mail is in this book.
Open the envelope. Take a look.

Or it may say

The Johnson mail is in this book.
Open the envelope. Take a look.

At child care or preschool, the book may have the name of each child, or it may have the name of the school; for example, "The Adams Hill School Mail Book." The verse would then say

The Adams Hill mail is in this book.
Open the envelope. Take a look.

★ Activity Instructions ★

Once again, use large pieces of construction paper for the front and back cover and for the pages inside the book, and print the poem on strips of paper or directly on the page. You may wish to use colored construction paper for the covers.

Each page has an envelope with the name of a different person. At school, there's a page for every child. If you wish to make a book like this at home, you could use the names of your child and his brothers and sisters and friends, other family members, or perhaps the names of dolls or action figures. Into each envelope, you can put a message for the person whose name is on it.

Preschool children eagerly open their envelopes to see the message. They quickly remember the predictable text on each page, and sometimes children want to add their own messages to the book.

If you're doing this at home, you can make the message shorter or longer, depending on your child's age. For instance, you might write, "I love you" or "Let's get juice" for a two-and-a-half-year-old. For a four-and-a-half-year-old you might write something slightly longer, such as "Our dog likes to play ball." Make sure you print your message in large, clearly written letters so it's easy for your child to make sense of them. This can be a whole-family activity, or you might do it with your child and several dolls or action figures.

As you turn each page, you might ask your child, "Whose message is in this envelope?" Children as young as toddlers sometimes recognize their own names, and as they get a bit older, they may also recognize the familiar names of others. If your child is beginning to associate sounds with letters, you might point out that Julia's name starts with a "j" and ask your child if he can think of another name that starts with that sound. If your child is beginning to recognize phonemes, you might ask if he can find a word that looks and sounds like the word (as you point at it) "book."

You can let your child pull out the message, and after you've read it once, you can invite your child to read it with you. You could also take dictation, writing down a message your child wants to send to someone else in the book, and then let him tuck the message into the appropriate envelope. If he's recognizing names, he may even be able to find the right envelope by himself.

As noted earlier, you can't really teach reading and writing separately, and this activity serves as an example. As you take dictation of your child's words and he watches you write them down, you're already encouraging writing. You can expand on this by giving him paper and pencil and letting him scribble or, if he's at that stage, write his own message.

You can expand on this activity by reading books about mail, such as *A Letter to Amy* by Ezra Jack Keats, and you can let your child help you open your own mail.

Ideas for Partnering with the Teacher or Provider

- If the preschool or child care has such a book, help your child send messages to put in the school's book. Write a message your child dictates, put it in an envelope, label it with the appropriate name, and let your child take the message to the center.

- Volunteer to make a mail book for the school or child care center.

- Alternatively, make a message center from a large piece of poster board and attach to it envelopes on which you've printed the children's names.

- Invite parents of other children at the center to help their children send messages to your child. You can then put them in her mail book. Or you could encourage your provider to have the children at the school or center write messages to your child.

> Old MacDonald Had a Farm

Old MacDonald Had a Farm is probably sung at your child's preschool or child care. Young children generally are captivated by animals, so they love to make the song's animal sounds. In fact, they often get quite excited about them. Another advantage of this activity is that the words are sung, which makes it easier for children to remember them. If your child already knows the words to this song, he may quickly begin to follow the print as you point at the words.

You can easily capitalize on this fanciful song at home with a big book. It can have as many or as few pages as you choose to give it.

★ Activity Instructions ★

On one sheet of construction paper, print the following words:

> *Old MacDonald had a farm,*
> *E – I – E – I – O*
> *And on his farm he had a dog,*
> *E – I – E – I – O.*

On a second sheet of construction paper, print the following words:

> *With a bowwow here,*
> *And a bowwow there,*
> *Here a bow,*
> *There a wow,*
> *Everywhere a bowwow.*

Make a pair of pages for each animal you want to include in your book. If your child is very young, start with just a few animals, perhaps three or four. You can add animals as both of you are ready. Print the words with a black marker, but use a different color for the names of the animals and their sounds. This helps children notice specific words and recognize that these are the words being spoken (voice-print pairing). Cut animal pictures from magazines, coloring books, or photographs and place an animal's picture on the page with the sound that animal makes.

As you read, you can ask questions and make comments to extend your child's thinking. For instance, you might ask, "What sound does a dog make?" or "Do you see that word anywhere?" or "Find two words that look the same (for example, 'moo, moo'). Let's see if they sound the same in the song." You can also pause at the end of a line and let your child fill in the word. For instance, you can say, "And on his farm he had a _____."

Your child may focus on the repetitious sounds the animal makes and notice that they look alike on the page. Some children will remember the spellings of some of the animal names, such as "cow" or "pig."

As you notice that your child can recognize sounds and associate them with letters, you can reinforce the learning she's doing. You might ask, "If we put the word 'horse' in the song, what sound would it start with?" Or say, "This animal's name starts with a 'p.'" Then make the sound several times before reading the word. Or you might ask, "What sound does the 'm' make in 'moo'?"

Even if you don't want to make a big book, you can still use these ideas at home or in similar activities at school. For instance, you could write out the names for each of your child's stuffed animals, "bear" or "cat" or "snake" or "pig," on index cards. Then ask her to bring a particular animal to you, sing the song with her, and show her the card that matches the name of the animal as you sing its name. You can expand on this by doing the same with the sound each animal makes.

Ideas for Partnering with the Teacher or Provider

- Let your child tell you the names of the animals and the sound each animal makes and then write each pair on a card. Your child can take the cards to the center for the teacher or provider to share with the other children when they sing the song.

- Let your child decorate a card with the name of an animal or its sound and then take cards she decorates to the center.

- Take the big book and your guitar (or banjo, or drums, or trombone) with you to school and sing the song with all the children. Your child could help you by turning the pages of your big book.

• • •

Summary of Partnering Ideas

- Talk with the teacher or provider about whether she's using big books at the center or family child care. If so, find out which big books she's using.

- Buy, or borrow from the library, regular versions of the books that are being used in big book form at the center or family child care.

- Ask your child about the big books she's reading at preschool or child care.

- See if you can borrow a big book from the center overnight and read it with your child at home.
- Take a big book you have at home to the center and read it with all the children.
- Offer to make a big book for the teacher or provider.
- Draw or paint a picture of the characters on the cover of a regular version of a big book and hang it in your child's room.
- Use magnetic letters to display on the refrigerator one or two of the important words from a big book.
- Let your child play with magnetic letters and help her form one or two important words from a big book.

Chapter 4
Words on the Wa

Many preschools and some child care settings use charts for children to interact with as they learn literacy skills. You can work with your child's teacher or provider to make this learning more meaningful. You might even want to make and use some charts at home. Your child will have fun with them while he's learning reading skills, and having charts at home will reinforce the skills he's learning at preschool or child care. At-home charts can include things going on in your child's setting, thereby helping your child feel the connections between home and preschool or child care and promoting his comfort there.

At home one day, Ahmed's father made a chart on which he drew a map of the neighborhood and put a cutout of a school right where the preschool was. Under the map he wrote: Every day _____ walks on _____ Street to get to school. And he made a card to fit in the blank that said "Ahmed," and another that said "Oak," since they lived on Oak Street. Ahmed loved the chart, and his father decided it would be fun to take it to school for all the children to play with. After the preschool

said she thought that was a great idea, he made
up cards with the names of all the children and the names
of all the streets they lived on. On the day Ahmed's father
came to preschool, he asked Ahmed to take the first turn.
Ahmed was so excited he could hardly contain himself.
His dad handed him the card with his name and he ran
to the chart. All the children loved the chart so much
that Ahmed's dad left it for the teacher to use. Besides
helping the children recognize their names, the chart also
helped them to better remember their addresses.

So what exactly is an interactive chart? It's a large piece
of paper with a poem, a song, or a saying, or snippets
from a favorite book—any text that is repetitive and predictable—written in large letters. It also has word cards
to insert at strategic places in the sentence to change its
meaning. So, if the chart said "Old MacDonald had a
farm," the word cards might say "House" and "Car" and
"Store." The teacher or provider could then change the
sentence to read "Old MacDonald had a house" or "Old
MacDonald had a car."

How Interactive Charts Help Children Learn

Interactive charts are a simple, powerful aid in teaching
children the foundational skills of reading. Besides building confidence, they teach essentially the same skills that
big books teach: phonemic awareness, that words have
boundaries, and that there's a relationship between a spoken word and a written word. Selecting words for the
word cards is critical. The words selected should both

change the meaning of the sentence *and* be significant to a child. They should, in other words, refer to something concrete and familiar or make an interesting or fun sound. Such words generally are a person's name, a noun, or an action verb. Young children soon lose interest if they are asked to match just any words. Generally, they don't stay interested in learning abstract words such as "old" or "had" or "a." If, however, a word has a purpose, refers to something they've seen, heard, tasted, or done, or, in the case of charts, fundamentally changes the meaning of a sentence, it becomes more valuable to them and sustains their interest.

How to Be a Partner with the Provider or Teacher in Using Charts

To build on your preschool or child care setting's use of interactive charts, find out what your child's teacher or child care provider is doing with this technique. Then create and use one or more of the same or similar interactive charts at home.

You can also incorporate school activities into charts you design at home. For instance, you could use the photos and names of other children at school in your chart. Or you might make a chart about a field trip, such as to an apple orchard, that your child has taken. If the center has a dress-up area with items such as fire and police hats, you might use a chart that talks about these roles.

You needn't make full-blown charts at home in order to reinforce what's happening at school. You could talk with the teacher or provider about home or family activities that are particularly important to your child and see whether she could integrate aspects of these activities into the charts she's working with. For instance, if your family goes ice skating together, she might be willing to make a chart that uses this activity. If your family recently went to the zoo, perhaps she could make a chart that talks about zoo animals.

You might ask the teacher or provider which words she's using in an interactive chart and then help your child make those words with magnetic letters at home. Or you might draw pictures with your child that represent the chart words he's playing with at school. If the chart is about food, you might serve the foods named on the chart. If it's a chart with words for various toys, you might make labels for the toys your child has at home that are the same as the words on the chart.

It's also possible that your child is not being exposed to interactive charts. This is especially likely if your child is in a family child care setting. You may want to suggest their use or even offer to make some charts for your provider. Remember, however, that she undoubtedly has her hands full and may not be able to add charts to her agenda. If this is the case, you can still use interactive charts at home if you wish.

>Choosing a Poem, Song, or Other Text for a Chart

Interactive charts should use poems or songs with repetitive words. Young children love repetition, and it makes the words easier to learn and remember. Poems and songs also should be relevant to their lives. In general, young children are interested in songs, poems, and books about children and their families, about farm and zoo animals, and about pets, weather, and other things that are part of their everyday lives. Your family and your child undoubtedly have unique interests that you can build on. Jenna's family, for example, loves to take wild-flower walks in the woods and identify the flowers, so an interactive chart with wildflowers as its subject would be perfect for Jenna.

If you're using a selection from a book, choose a specific sentence that is repeated throughout the book. An example is *Owl Babies* by Martin Waddell, which repeats the sentence "'I want my mommy,' said Bill." (Your child's name would substitute for "Bill," of course.)

Generally, a chart should have no more than four to six lines. If your child is younger than three, the chart should probably have one- or two-line poems or songs.

The most important written words for young children are their names, so charts that allow them to recognize and handle their written-out names are especially motivating. Other words of high interest—color words, animal names, and the names of characters in books they love—can be added in new charts. The names of items children use when they're playing, such as "hammer" or "saw" or "stove" or "fork," are also good choices. Generally, you want to use nouns or, in the case of color words, adjectives. Avoid words that are abstract and difficult to illustrate, such as "windy" or "big" or "happy."

Can Young Children Actually Read the Words on Word Cards?

Young children quickly recognize their names, or at least

the first letters of their names. In the past, people assumed young children couldn't recognize their names until they could read. Teachers would often use a symbol, such as an apple or a carrot, next to a child's name to help him recognize his own name card. We now know that even young children usually don't need symbols; they do learn to recognize their printed names. They can also learn to recognize other types of words, but they need picture cues to help them learn the words. So, if a word card says "hammer," it should include a picture of a hammer.

Using a Chart at Home

If you decide to use a chart at home, hang it on the wall in a place where it's easy to talk about and play with— perhaps in the kitchen so you and your child can use it when you're cooking, especially if it's a chart that relates in some way to food. Or you might hang it in your child's bedroom or on the wall of a playroom.

Leave the chart in place for two or three weeks. Children need to be able to return to a chart many times in order to develop their theories about reading and writing. When they have extensive opportunities to interact with the print on charts, children pay closer attention to the details of individual letters and words, notice word boundaries, and create letter and sound relationships.

When you've used a chart for a while at home, you could offer to send it to preschool or child care, where your child could share it with his friends, and maybe even be able to "teach." Besides being fun for him, it

would also be a confidence booster. You also could
with the teacher or provider about allowing activitie
school related to a chart you're using at home. For insta   ‿,
if you're using a chart about food at home, your child
could bring in snack-size portions of a food identified on
your chart.

There are many kinds of charts you can use at home.
An ideal one is a job chart, which you'd start by listing
the jobs the children in your family are assigned, such as
feeding the fish or sweeping the porch, and then adding
the appropriate name after each job. Or, starting with
dates and names, you could create a happy birthday chart
for family members.

How to Make an Interactive Chart

You can make an interactive chart with poster board,
which comes in white and many colors. Buy it at any
art supply store or at a drugstore. You can use water-
color markers to write directly on the poster board, but
choose markers with pointed rather than flat tips.
Pointed tips are best for making large letters. Avoid
permanent markers, which sometimes bleed through
the paper and make lines that are too thin. You can
find sentence strips in school-supply catalogs or school-
supply stores and sometimes in craft stores. These
strips of paper with lines on them guide your writing;
they come in white, manila, and pastel colors. Write on
the strips and then glue them to the poster board.
Write your letters in a standard, easy-to-read form.
Make sure you leave plenty of space between words so

it's easy to see where they begin and end.

Add pictures, photos, or drawings that illustrate the words. Such additions act as cues that help children figure out what a word says. For example, if you're making a chart about eating an apple pie, you might cut out pictures of apples or flour. If you're making a chart about going to the zoo, you might look for zoo animal stickers to decorate your chart.

Color can be an important part of a chart. For instance, if you're making a chart with lines from a certain book, you can use the color scheme from the book. This would help children associate the chart with the book and so would help them remember the words more easily. You want the letters to be easy to read, so black writing on white paper generally is a good choice. Yellow marker is too light to read. Black marker on bright yellow sentence strips gives high contrast, which is helpful to a child with a visual disability.

Finally, print the key words on cards. The print on your cards should match the print on the poster, both in size and in color, so the cards fit in flawlessly when you're reading. Print your key words on small index cards or on sentence strips. To make everything more durable, you may want to laminate the poster board and the cards when you're finished.

Sample Activities

> The Train

A great thing about this chart is that it builds on your child's interest in his name and the names of other children. Made in the shape of a train, the chart has a window in the engine where photos can be inserted. The verse printed under the window says:

> *I looked in the engine*
> *And what did I see?*
> *I saw* _____
> *Looking back at me.*

Your child can insert her photo into the window, and then add her name to the poem printed on the engine. She can also add the photos and names of her classmates, friends, or family.

★ Activity Instructions ★

Cut the shape of the train engine out of black poster board and use a gold metallic marker to write the words. Then laminate the train and, using clear acetate, extra lamination film, or packing tape, make a pocket for holding photos. Make name cards by printing the names on heavy paper or index cards and then laminating them. Attach magnetic tape, which generally comes in rolls, to the chart and to the name cards so they'll stick to the chart. Two strips of the tape stick together because of magnetic attraction, and the backs of both tapes have adhesive covered by peel-off paper. Cut the tape strips into appropriate lengths. Once you peel off the paper backing, the tape will permanently adhere to whatever surface you press it against. Magnetic tape can be found at craft stores and sometimes at fabric stores.

Read the engine verse with your child, pointing to

each word as you read it. Then pause to let your child insert her photo and place her name on the chart. She can also insert photos of other children or family members or other people who are important to her and place their names on the chart.

As she becomes familiar with the poem, your child may want to say it aloud with you and even point to the words herself. She'll need help finding matching names at first, but she'll eventually start to recognize them. When you notice that she's beginning to recognize her name and the names of others, you can ask her to find the name that matches a photo. She may compare the way the names look as she moves them about.

After a while you can also point out names that start with the same letter. You can encourage your child's phonetic awareness by such things as pointing out that "see" and "saw" begin with the same sound. You can ask what word sounds like "see." Or, with an older child, you can observe, "The word *engine* begins with the letter 'e,' but when I say the word I hear the name for the letter 'n.'" You might want to make charts with other kinds of vehicles—cars, airplanes, or boats, for example.

Ideas for Partnering with the Teacher or Provider

- Take digital photos of class members (get permission from each family first) and add them to your home chart.
- If your preschool or child care doesn't have the chart described on the next page, you and your child could make one.

❯ Chicka Chicka Boom Boom

This chart uses a traditional chant from *Chicka Chicka Boom Boom,* by Bill Martin Jr. and John Archambault, to introduce young children to alphabet letters. The chart has a giant felt coconut tree on which alphabet letters can be placed. Under the tree are the words of the chant:

> *Chicka chicka boom boom*
> *Will there be enough room*
> *For _____ and _____*
> *Up the coconut tree?*

Your child can insert individual letters of the alphabet in the blanks and put the same letters on the tree.

★ Activity Instructions ★

For this chart, use blue poster board to suggest sky in the background. Use a gold marker to write the verse directly on the bottom half of the poster board,

or use white sentence strips and attach them to the poster board. After laminating the poster, cut out a giant felt coconut tree (use brown felt for the tree trunk and the coconuts and green felt for the palm fronds) and, using rubber cement, attach it to the poster above the verse. Cut two sets of uppercase alphabet letters from construction paper and attach self-adhesive Velcro to the back of each letter. Attach Velcro to the corresponding places on the poster. With Velcro, letters can be attached to the poster easily.

At first your child may simply want to play with the letters without reading the chart. You might start by asking him to choose some letters to put on the tree while you name the letters he chooses. When he's ready to pay attention, read the chant to him, pausing at the blanks so he can pick out a letter to insert. Do this over and over again, giving him many chances to pick out different letters. Again, each time he chooses a letter, say its name aloud. Your child may eventually want to read the chart with you and say the names of the letters himself.

When he chooses a letter for one of the blanks, you may want to ask if he can find the same letter to put on the tree. Or you could ask him to move the letter on the tree and then read the chant again, asking him to choose additional letters for the blanks.

You could also ask him to look for the letter that his name begins with. If he knows how to spell his name, he may want to look for all the letters in it. Remember that you'll need to make additional letters if any letter in your child's name is used more than once. With this chart, you can elaborate as your child is ready by helping him spell other names or words he's interested in.

Questions you can ask your child to help him extend his thinking include "Which letter will run to the coconut tree first?" "Can you find all the letters for your name?" "Can you help me find the letters for my name."

You can encourage your child's awareness of phonemes with instructions such as "Look at the 'c' and the 'k' in 'chicka.' Together they make the 'kuh' sound." Or "What sounds do you hear in 'boom'? The two 'o's together make a sound. Listen as I say the word again."

Ideas for Partnering with the Teacher or Provider

- Take the chart to preschool or child care and lead the activity with the children.
- Let the teacher or provider use the chart.
- Use the letters from the chart to spell your child's name and the names of other children at the school or center.
- Get foam alphabet letters for your child to play with, and share them with the school or center.

>Bingo Revisited

This chart is derived from the popular children's song "Bingo." The words to the song are printed on the chart, leaving a blank space to fill in a name. In place of "B-I-N-G-O," children spell out their own name and the names of others and sing them as they read the chart.

Cutout shapes (silhouettes) of children dance across the top of the chart. Under the figures are the four lines of the song:

> *There is a child at our school*
> *Can you guess the name, oh,*
>
> _____
>
> *and _____ is the name, oh.*

If you're using this chart at home, you'll want to replace the first line with "There is a child at our house."

★ Activity Instructions ★

Use colored or white poster board. You can buy silhouette stickers of children at school-supply stores, craft stores, or drugstores, or you can cut your own out of colored construction paper. Glue the silhouettes across the top of the chart. Beneath them, in a contrasting color, print the words to the song, either directly on the poster board or on sentence strips. Attach strips of self-adhesive magnetic tape in the blank spaces.

Cut out small squares of construction paper. Then write, one letter per square, the letters of each name you want available for your child to put on the poster board. In addition, write each entire name on a strip of paper or a sentence strip that can be inserted into the last line of the song. Attach adhesive magnetic tape to the backs of the letters and names and to the appropriate places on the chart. Store each name in a separate envelope. On the outside of the envelope, write the name in large, clear letters.

If you're using this chart at home, you can use the names of your child's classmates or other friends or the names of family members or other relatives. You could also use the names of your child's dolls or pets or the names of action heroes or storybook characters she likes.

Sing the song with your child until it's easy for her to remember it. Then ask her to attach the letters for her (or some other) name to the chart as you sing the song together. During that first round, you'll need to hand her the correct envelope for the name she's chosen to go on the chart. Eventually she may begin to pick out the right envelope by herself. You can invite her to do this if you think she's recognizing the name, but don't push her. Depending on her experience level, she'll probably also need help arranging and attaching the letters.

As you play together, you can ask questions to help your child think about the letters, words, and sounds. For instance, you could ask, "Whose name starts with a 'k'?" Or say, "I found the 'b.' What other letters will I need for 'Briana'?" You can encourage phonetic awareness by asking questions such as "Which name starts with the same sound as 'Caitlyn'?" or "Which letter makes the sound at the end of 'Will'?"

Ideas for Partnering with the Teacher or Provider

- Make up envelopes with the names of each of your child's classmates and use them in your chart at home.

- Also for your chart at home, make up envelopes with the names of the teachers or providers and other staff at the center.

- Take your chart to school and introduce the activity to your child's classmates.

• • •

Summary of Partnering Ideas

- Ask the teacher or provider if she's using interactive charts. If so, ask which charts she's using.

- Make the same or similar interactive charts at home.

- Offer to make interactive charts for the preschool or child care.

- Go to the center or family child care and lead an activity with an interactive chart.

- Incorporate school activities into charts you use at home. For example, use the photos and names of other children at the school, or make a chart about a field trip they've taken.

- See if the teacher or provider can incorporate important home activities into her school's charts.

- Use magnetic letters at home to spell out words being used on the school's or center's word cards.

- Draw with your child pictures that represent items from word cards on the charts he's playing with at child care or preschool.

Chapter 5
Words All Around Us

Our culture depends on the written word to function, so it's easy to find words in our daily lives to point out and read to children. We have to read highway signs to drive, read labels at the grocery store to know what we're buying and how much it costs, read instructions for the new tool or gadget we've bought, read the follow-up instructions after taking a sick child to the doctor, read updates on storm warnings or highway construction or on changes being made to daylight saving time. We're surrounded by words.

In preschools and child care centers, the words all around us that we ask children to notice and use to help them learn to read are called *environmental print*—literally, the printed words in our environment.

Environmental print serves as a wonderful example of using all parts of the environment as potential curriculum content to teach reading and writing. It helps children make sense of words that have meaning for them and therefore helps motivate them to learn. And what could have more meaning for a child than recognizing her name printed above the special hook for her coat, or being able to read the message on the refrigerator that says, "Katya, I love you. Mom" or the sign at the pet store that says, "Kittens for sale."

Preschools and child care centers have many ways of taking advantage of environmental print, ways that provide rich opportunities for you to collaborate with your child's provider or teacher.

How Environmental Print Helps Children Learn

Environmental print teaches the same basic reading skills taught by interactive charts and big books, but it can be especially motivating because it can help children interpret the daily world they inhabit, allowing them to both enjoy it more completely and function in it more successfully. When children can recognize their names on holiday gift packages, reading holds obvious purpose for them. It becomes very useful, when they have to go to the bathroom, to recognize the words "Girls" and "Boys." When they're helping mom or dad shop, being able to distinguish between different products in the grocery store will matter a lot to them. Having the meanings of words in the environment pointed out makes it concrete to a young child that words do, indeed, have a function.

Environmental print also offers a great opportunity for positive modeling as, for example, you and your child's teacher show how helpful reading is when you use recipes or look up a phone number or read directions.

How to Be a Partner with the Provider or Teacher in Using Environmental Print

Teachers and providers often use the existing print in children's environments as a teaching tool. They'll point out, for instance, traditional signs such as "Exit," "Stop," or "Detour," as well as the labels on food packages. They'll point out important words on field trips. A teacher might point out the sign that says, "Don't feed the bears," at the zoo. As she walks with the children to the library, the provider might point out the sign that says "Stop."

Teachers and providers also design environmental print to include in the classroom. They might put the children's names on their cubbies, place a "Closed" sign in a certain curriculum area at certain times of the day, put up labels and signs to organize shelves, list names on attendance charts, list jobs next to names, or make signs for dramatic play areas. A preschool's kitchen area might be called "Pizza Parlor" one week and "Café" the next. A provider might put up a message board with a new message each day, or a billboard with a word that labels the day's weather as "Sunny" or "Rainy" or "Cloudy" or "Snowy." She might include toy road signs in the block area or small menus in the kitchen area.

If, as you take your child to school, you read big signs along the way that might matter to your child, perhaps "Library" or "Toy Store," you'll reinforce the work your teacher or provider is doing. You might read aloud the street sign where the school is located as you arrive at school and mention to the teacher or provider that you and your child read it that day. If your child's cubby or coat hook is labeled with his name, read his name aloud, or ask him to read it to you.

You could look at the labels on art shelves or toy shelves at school and use similar ones at home. Check out the dramatic play areas and the words they contain and see if there's a way you could repeat them at home. Ask your provider if she could use some of the magazines you subscribe to that would be appropriate for your child's dramatic play areas. At one center, a mother brought old copies of *Ranger Rick* that the teacher then put in the doctor's waiting room play area. Perhaps the teacher or provider would like empty food containers for the play area, and you could send a few from your child's favorite foods—macaroni and cheese, perhaps, or yogurt or peanut butter.

When Sergio's father sent birthday treats to the child care center, he wrote a card for each child. On index cards, he'd printed, "Cupcake for Debbie," "Cupcake for Kyle," and so on. The staff at the center were delighted to read each child's card, and several of the children saved their cards. If you're sending birthday treats to the center, think up a label of some kind to send with your child. Another idea is to find out what food will be served the next day and make a menu to send with your child. You might even make photocopies of it so your child can hand out menus to all his classmates. Or ask for the recipe for your child's favorite food at school, make up a recipe card, and prepare the food at home. You can also brainstorm with the teacher or provider about ways to partner. She might appreciate your making up some signs for school and you could enlist your child's help in creating them. Or ask for your child's help in choosing empty food containers or magazines to send to school.

Taking Advantage of Environmental Print at Home

You can multiply the use of environmental print in many ways at home. You might, for instance, label your child's toothbrush or other personal items with her name. You could make place cards for family members that your child can put on the table. Give your child play money to use when she plays "restaurant" or "going to the store" with friends. You can use "Open" and "Closed" signs on a playroom or a television or on other areas or appliances that your children use at home. You might even put a sign on the bathroom door that says "Occupied" on one side and "Vacant" on the other. You can ask your child to look in the newspaper for a coupon for his favorite food.

You can help your child mount birthday and holiday cards in a special scrapbook that the two of you can read and reread. Carefully print on the calendar events that are important to your child—"Picnic," for example, or "Grandma's birthday"—and periodically point them out to her. If your child sometimes helps you cook, point out the words in a recipe book or the directions on a cake box. Occasionally send a special note or postcard to your child through the mail. Nothing is more exciting to a young child than receiving her own mail.

Sample Activities

Described below are some examples of activities using environmental print at preschool, at child care, and at home, and some ideas about how you might reinforce what your child is learning at school.

＞ The Job Chart

Job charts can provide a common theme between home and school. In many early childhood classrooms or child care homes or centers, children take turns feeding the fish, watering the plants, or doing other tasks, such as setting the table or sweeping the floor after lunch. These tasks afford an ideal opportunity to encourage reading.

★ Activity Instructions ★

At the center, the teacher or provider may have a poster board with a question such as "Do you have a job today?" printed across the top. On the next line, the words might say, "Set up lunch" and be accompanied by a picture of children eating at a table. Next to the line there may be a pocket made with clear laminating film in which a card with a child's name on it could be placed. Another line, this one saying "Feed the fish," might be accompanied by a picture of a fish and have a pocket to hold another child's name.

You can make a similar chart at home using the same kinds of material used in interactive charts. First write out your list of jobs—Pick up toys, Make your bed, and so on. Then make up name cards for your preschooler, as well as for any older children you have. Although your older children may show no interest in the chart, your preschooler may be interested in seeing his siblings' names on the chart along with his own. If you have no other children, you could include tasks that grown-ups do, along with name cards that say "Mommy" or "Daddy" or "Grandpa" or "Aunt Mae" or whoever those persons are in your family.

After you post your chart—perhaps by the breakfast table—your child probably will begin looking for his name on the chart, first identifying it by its first letter. At some point he'll be able to identify the other names, once again probably only by the first letter in the beginning. As you look at the chart with your child, you can ask him questions such as, "Do you have a job today?" or "Whose turn is it to feed the dog today? How can you find out?"

If two family members have names that begin with the same letter, you can say to your child, "'Marcus' and 'Michela' both begin with the same letter. How do you know which name card says 'Marcus' and which says 'Michela'?" Asking such a question encourages phonetic awareness.

Ideas for Partnering with the Teacher or Provider

- Ask your child about the jobs she does at school.

- Add to your home chart a job that your child can do at school or at the provider's house, perhaps helping clear the lunch dishes.

- Check out what play themes—firefighter or doctor, perhaps—are being used at school or at the provider's house. Then make a pretend job chart of responsibilities for an appropriate worker.

>Daily Message Board

Providers and teachers often write a daily message on a message board. They may use the board to describe the art activity for the day, to announce a special visitor, or to remind children to return field trip permission forms.

★ Activity Instructions ★

You can use a message board at home as well. Simply buy a small dry-erase board and some dry-erase markers and place the board where your child can see it. You might put it where he sees it in the morning before he leaves, or near the door where he walks in at the end of the day. Wherever you decide to put it, make sure you place it at your child's eye level.

Change the message each day. It might be a message from a grandparent: "Grandpa says hello." It might be a message from you: "Have a good day" or "Wear your mittens." If a parent is traveling, the message board provides an ideal place for contact: "Daddy called. He loves you." Or "Mommy will call after school."

You can also include messages about what you'll be doing later in the day or about expected visitors: "Vang is coming over." Or "Today we will go to the library." Or you can use your message board for reminders: "Make a card for Leah."

Ideas for Partnering with the Teacher or Provider

- Read the message board at the center aloud with your child.
- When your child gets home, begin the day's transition by

joining her at the art activity announced on the provider's message board, or by talking about the person who visited preschool that morning.

- When your child comes home, ask her what was written on the center's message board that day.
- Post at home messages related to the preschool or child care center. "Draw me a picture at school" might be one of your messages.

>Fruit Salad

This activity uses single-recipe booklets that focus children's attention on print while they cook. One step of a very simple recipe is written on each page of a booklet.

★ Activity Instructions ★

You can make a simple recipe booklet using index cards. On each card, write one simple instruction, such as, "Slice one banana." Illustrate the cards and laminate them or cover them with clear self-adhesive paper. Punch a hole in the upper left corner of each card and join the cards together with a small metal circle like those used to hold keys or with ribbon. If you use ribbon, tie it loosely enough that the pages can be turned without binding.

Your child can make a fruit salad recipe under your supervision. If he can read, you might ask him to read the sentence on each card before he follows the directions. If he's not yet ready to read sentences, you could read them to him, pointing at each word as you read. Let him read aloud any words he recognizes.

As your child cooks, you might make comments or ask questions that focus on your printed words. "I'll add the peach to our salad," you might say. "What sound does 'peach' start with?" Or "Listen to the end of 'peach.' 'C' and 'h' go together to make that sound."

You could also ask if he wants to add any other kind of fruit to the salad. Then let him watch as you make up a card with the instruction for adding that fruit to your recipe booklet. If he's able to write the words, or any of the letters, see if he wants to help you.

Most any simple recipe can be used in making a booklet. English-muffin pizzas are easy to make, and pistachio pudding, made from a package, surprises children by turning green when they add milk. You might cut out the front of the pudding package and use it as the cover of that recipe booklet.

Ideas for Partnering with the Teacher or Provider

- Using a single-recipe booklet, cook something with your child and send the food to preschool or child care to share. (This may be impossible if local regulations require that any food brought to a center for sharing be purchased.)

- Let your child take a single-recipe booklet to school. Your child could share it during circle time, or perhaps it could be used to cook the item there.

- Find out what foods served at preschool or child care your child particularly likes and help your child create a single-recipe booklet for that food.

• • •

Summary of Partnering Ideas

- Talk with your child's teacher or provider about how she uses environmental print and then make the same or similar environmental print to use at home.

- On the way to preschool or child care, read aloud important signs, such as "Library" or "Toy Store," or the street signs.

- Offer to make environmental print for your child's preschool or child care. Involve your child in making it.

- Let your child help you choose empty containers for her favorite foods to send to school, or ask her to help pick out family magazines to send to her child care center for dramatic play.

- Write messages about preschool or child care on your message board at home.

- Make menus of school or center lunches. Send one of the menus with your child, or make photocopies so she can give one to each child.

- Let your child bring a snack for all the children. Write the name of the snack on its packaging in large, clear letters.

- Make a recipe card your child can take to school.

Chapter 6
Early Writing

Connie was sitting at her kitchen table looking through a tattered old cardboard box that was decorated with a child's drawings. In that box, Connie's mother had collected pictures Connie drew at preschool, her report cards, even the place cards she'd made for Thanksgiving when she was seven years old.

Connie hadn't looked in this box for years, but now that her four-year-old son was bringing home his own pictures from preschool, she decided to make a similar one for him. She giggled quietly at a cat she'd drawn that was mostly a head. Her mom had labeled it, "Boots, by Connie, age 5." Connie unfolded a large piece of paper with scattered groups of colorful, painstakingly drawn circles. Some were full circles, some were tiny, and many of them had a break or distortion where her young fingers hadn't succeeded in guiding the marker all the way through closing her circle. Another piece of paper bore what looked at first like writing but proved to be just careful little circles and lines, hills and valleys.

Those meticulous scrawls reminded Connie of the markings her son had made earlier that morning while she was cleaning up the kitchen after breakfast. Because she'd attended a parents' meeting at Jared's preschool the night before, she'd been able to recognize those marks as an early attempt at writing. A teacher at the meeting had talked about how young children learn to read and write, about what she was doing in the classroom to encourage early reading and writing, and about what parents could do at home to bolster it.

After a nostalgic hour enjoying her childhood papers, Connie decided to hunt for a sturdy box for Jared to decorate. But first she dug out the paper on which he'd written his "sentences" that morning. She labeled it "Sentences, by Jared, age 4" and put it up on the refrigerator.

When young children play with pencils and paper, they are making their earliest attempts at producing words on paper. Children can become interested in writing as early as about three years of age, at the time when they're coordinated enough to control a pencil or marker. They cannot, of course, form recognizable words or even letters, but they are becoming aware of written language and will experiment with mimicking it in increasingly sophisticated ways.

Writing Activities at Child Care or Preschool

Preschools and child care centers use a variety of methods to encourage young children's interest in writing and in experimenting with it. These range from the formal methods built into the curriculums to the more informal interactions and activities providers or teachers may employ at their own discretion. Preschools are more apt to set aside specific areas for writing, areas that have a small table and paper, pencils, crayons, and markers. Such areas may also have blank books or fill-in-the-blank papers, and they may be organized around themes such as seasons or holidays. In such a setting, journal writing time, mail time, and other opportunities for writing are structured into a child's days. Even if child care centers and family child care providers don't have space for permanent writing centers, they can still offer many opportunities for writing. These can vary from notes carried to and from home that include a child's writing, to a child labeling her own artwork, to more formal writing activities built into a weekly schedule.

No matter what kind of child care setting your son or daughter is in, it's important that you understand the ways in which writing emerges in your child, how you can encourage it, and how you can enrich this experience by collaborating with your child's teacher or provider.

How Writing Emerges

Before children can use letters as symbols that communicate thoughts—which is what writing is—they have to understand that print has a specific meaning. Children's early experiments with writing help them to understand the concepts related to writing, such as the fact that words are made up of a particular sequence of letters. These early efforts lay the foundation for understanding more sophisticated concepts, such as the function of capital letters and punctuation marks.

Writing emerges in young children in predictable stages, which can begin with scribbling as early as age three, with the last stages of writing letters and words progressing into the early school years. If you watch closely, you can see a pattern of development in your child's early writing.

The first stage is *scribbling*. Though similar to their first scribblings in art, the marks children make when they first "write" are more controlled. What they produce is akin to the babbling sounds they make when they first experiment with talking. Babbling lets children explore sounds. Scribbling lets them explore the visual appearance of writing.

Stage 1 Examples: Scribbling

The second stage, called *linear/repetitive drawing* or *personal cursive*, is a sort of refined version of scribbling. As children learn to speak, they gradually drop sounds from their babbling that aren't part of the words in their own language. Similarly, as they learn to write, they become increasingly aware of how writing actually looks and they refine their own attempts. During this stage their scribbling starts to look a lot more like actual writing. In fact, teachers who aren't familiar with a child's native language may mistake a child's personal cursive for actual writing.

Stage 2 Examples: Personal Cursive

During stage three, called *letter-like forms,* children draw marks that look very close to printing. Sometimes, in fact, actual letters are intermingled in their writing.

Stage 3 Examples: Letter-like Forms

In stage four, known as *letters and early word–symbol relationships,* children begin to reproduce letters, often using them to represent whole words. If a child is writing a group of words, she may use a different letter or letter-like form for each "word" she writes. This approach is similar to early speech, when children use one word to represent an entire thought, such as "eat" for "I'm hungry."

During stage five, called *invented spelling,* children

Stage 4 Example: Word–Symbol Relationships

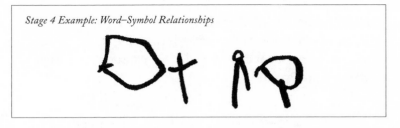

generally begin by using just one consonant to represent a word and then proceed toward using additional consonants to represent a word. Not every word will contain a letter to represent each consonant in that word, and a child may use the wrong consonant for a sound, but it's clear that he's starting to understand the structure of words. A child at the beginning of this stage, may write a message using mostly consonants. If he writes the same message several weeks later, it will have more vowels, even though they may not be the correct vowels. The errors children make in writing during this stage are similar to the overgeneralizations they make as they learn to speak, such as saying "mouses" for "mice."

Stage 5 Examples: Invented Spelling

At stage six, called *standard spelling,* children begin to remember the spelling of familiar words. This can happen even in preschool. They may, however, still revert to earlier stages of writing when they have a lot to say. What you're most likely to see during this stage is long strands of personal cursive or letter-like forms punctuated by actual words.

Stage 6 Examples: Standard Spelling

I Want to Sit Next to Daniel W

I LIKe ice Cream And The Butter Fly IS Back

Working with Teachers and Providers to Encourage Writing

Preschools and child care centers generally use a variety of ways to encourage young children to experiment, ways that you can build on at home. You can, of course, talk with your child's teacher or provider about how she encourages writing and ask for her advice on what you can do at home to complement her efforts. You can also ask her for feedback on what stage in his writing development your child is at.

Teachers and providers sometimes keep both notes that describe each child's writing progress and examples of writing from throughout the year. Some keep portfolios, which means they keep a folder for each child. A teacher's notes on a particular writing incident would include details such as which hand the child used, how the child held the pencil or marker, what stage of writing appeared, how long the child engaged in writing, and where in the classroom the writing took place.

If your child's teacher or provider does not keep notes, you may want to ask her if she can monitor your child's writing in this way and give you feedback, or send home examples that you can save yourself. Keep in mind, however, that it may be impossible for your provider to do this, especially if your child is in a family child care. She may simply have too many young children to monitor, or she may not be trained in recognizing the specific stages of writing. If the latter is true of your provider, she may be interested in any information you can provide her, but again, it's important to remember that she has limits on her time. If you want more structured curriculum and teaching than your provider can give you, you may want to investigate other centers or preschools in your community to see what kinds of programs are available.

The good news is that no matter what kind of child care setting you've chosen for your child—formal or informal, structured or not very structured—there are important things you can do to assist the provider or teacher in enriching your child's experience.

Dos and Don'ts

First and foremost, we adults need to accept all writing attempts as legitimate. In other words, just as we respond to a baby's babbling because it's a real form of communication, we need to acknowledge that a young child's first writing is a real attempt to communicate. With encouragement, a child continues to experiment with the writing process. A teacher or provider might, for example, say, "I see a lot of writing underneath your picture." Or, "Tell me what you were thinking about when you wrote this." As a parent, you might do what Connie did when she saw Jared's first scribbling: label it as writing and display it with pride. You might also take your child's proud scribblings to her preschool or child care center to share with her teacher or provider.

It's also important that you don't push your child faster than he's ready to go, which can cause unnecessary frustration and discourage your child from trying to write. Remember that young children need many chances to experiment with writing materials before they're actually coordinated enough to produce particular strokes.

Both you and your child's teacher or provider also need to accept your child's pencil grasp. Remember that during the early stages of writing, a child holds a pencil in a way that's comfortable for her. As she gradually develops more hand and finger strength and better coordination, she will change her grip.

Just as there are names for the stages of learning to write, there are names for the stages most young children go through in grasping a pencil or marker. The first is a *fist grip,* in which a child wraps all four fingers around a pencil. Some children wrap all four fingers around the pencil *and* rotate their hand so that the back of their hand faces away from their body in an *overhand grip.* Later on, many children develop a *three-finger grip,* with two fingers on top of the pencil and the thumb opposing them. In a *tripod grip,* the most mature grasp and the standard writing position, one finger is on top of the pencil, one is below the pencil, and the thumb opposes them. Many older preschool children hold a pencil with a tripod grip, but don't worry if your child doesn't. Some children continue to hold a pencil near the eraser end for a while, and some kindergarteners still use a fist grip.

If you can tell that your child is frustrated as he tries to write because of the way he's holding the pencil, you can show him another way to hold it. Just make sure that what you offer is a suggestion, not an ultimatum. Insisting that a child hold a pencil a certain way, especially if it's uncomfortable for him, may discourage him from trying to write at all.

Preschools and child care centers generally keep lots of different writing materials at hand, and this is a good idea at home as well. Younger children often feel more comfortable writing with a marker than with a pencil since they may not yet have enough finger strength to create a dark mark with a pencil. On the other hand, because they see adults writing with pencils, they often are eager to try them. The more experience children have with pencils and other writing devices, the stronger their fingers become. And you don't need to give your child "fat" pencils. When given a choice, children often prefer regular-width pencils to the wider ones.

Keep both lined and unlined paper around. Young children's first attempts at writing are usually large shaky forms that they place randomly across a piece of paper. Since they can't fit letters neatly between lines, lined paper may be intimidating for them. Later, when they begin to refine their writing and gain better control, lined paper provides a useful guide for their writing.

Many centers have computers available for young children. A computer can also be a good tool for encouraging writing at home. Young children will begin by using the keyboard to type random letters, a stage that can last a long time. Then they may begin to type one particular letter to represent a whole word, often the first letter of their name. Soon they'll begin leaving spaces between groups of letters to simulate words. Such early use of a computer encourages comfort with a tool that is rapidly becoming indispensable.

• • •

Tools and Activities to Encourage Writing

Listed below are some of the tools and activities that teachers and child care providers use to encourage writing. In the following chapters, you'll find many examples of how the activities briefly described here can be used to encourage writing.

- *Writing centers.* These are specific areas that encourage writing by providing interesting writing materials and appropriate models.
- *Class books.* Children can contribute an individual page to a class book.
- *Pocket stories.* Children dictate a sentence to go with a picture they create. Duplicate words can be matched to the words in their sentence and stored in the pocket at the bottom of the page.

- *Writing caddies.* Boxes or other containers holding basic writing materials, such as paper, pencils, and markers, are placed around the classroom or center to encourage writing everywhere.

- *Sentence fill-ins.* Children experiment with writing by adding a word or phrase to a predictable text.

- *Journal writing.* This activity book, which is common in many classrooms and centers, allows staff to trace children's writing progress.

- *Writing on interactive charts.* By changing a word on a chart, children can experiment with the way writing conveys meaning.

- *Literary suitcases.* Typically plastic boxes or backpacks, this kind of suitcase generally contains a children's book and related writing materials.

In the next three chapters, we'll take a closer look at some early writing activities that are typical of those used in preschools and in some child care centers and family child care homes.

Chapter 7
Writing Explorations

You don't have to teach your child to write. All you have to do is give her a little encouragement—and that can be as simple as being sure she sees see you write. Luckily, writing is so much a part of our world that our children get a chance to see us using this skill every day. We write grocery lists and letters, fill out forms, take phone messages, and on and on. And it's easy to get a child involved: Just put out some paper and pencils or markers and let your child "write" next to you.

You can also develop activities based on the writing that occurs at home every day and on the writing activities that take place at preschool or child care. Some of the common activities preschools and many child care centers and family day care homes use to encourage writing explorations are examined below.

How Writing Exploration Activities Help Children Learn

As we discussed earlier, learning to write begins before children even know their ABCs. Writing exploration activities teach essentially the same skills that reading activities teach: confidence, the understanding that there is a relationship between the spoken word and the written word, word boundaries, and phonetic awareness. Writing activities such as dictating stories or creating scrapbooks help children understand the fundamental concept that print has meaning. Writing exploration activities also help young children learn the specific mechanics of writing, such as the need for a particular sequence of letters in order to form specific words. The developmental progression of young children's writing is reflected in the techniques that centers use to encourage writing.

> Taking Dictation

For instance, a center might help children to write notes to a parent and may encourage parents to help children write notes back to them. The adult begins by writing down on a note card what the child says. The child then might sign his name, although at this stage, his signature is likely to be a scribble. The next step—when the child is ready (usually around age four or five)—might be to encourage him to copy the name of the person he's writing to. At some point, the child will begin to write some of the words on the cards himself.

Taking dictation, which doesn't require a permanent space, lends itself to all types of settings, from preschools to family child care homes. As teachers and providers write down the stories that young children dictate, children begin to understand the relationship between written and spoken language. This can be a natural bridge to actual writing.

Parents can write down their children's stories as well. Following the lead of knowledgeable teachers and providers, you should be careful to write exactly what your child says, even when she makes grammatical errors. If you make corrections in what she says, she'll be looking at a printed representation that is different from what she said, which may be confusing for her. If, for instance, your child says, "The wind blowed," and you write it as "The wind blew," the words as sounded out won't match up with the words as represented on paper. You needn't worry that writing down what she says even when it's not grammatically correct will reinforce bad grammar. It won't. You and your child's teacher or provider will still model correct grammar when you talk to her. Keep in mind that the goal of taking dictation is to help children construct an accurate understanding of the relationship between spoken and written language.

Seeing their words written down encourages young children to begin writing themselves. Print clearly and in a standard form that closely resembles the print your child sees when he looks at books. You can share the stories your child dictates to you with the teacher or provider, who can, in turn, talk with your child about the stories he invents at home. You might also write stories as a family, especially when you're traveling. A parent can start the story, and it can go in many directions. For instance, a parent might start by saying, "One day I went to the beach. At the beach I played in the water. I saw a jellyfish float by." Then another family member takes up the story. With a clipboard as a writing surface, you can take your child's dictation or, if your child is ready, he can write down some of the words in the story. When you return from your trip, your child may wish to take your family's story to preschool or child care.

>Documenting Activities with Journal Writing and Scrapbooks

Many teachers and providers make journal writing a regular part of the class schedule or make it available whenever children are interested. Sometimes teachers or providers make journal folders for each child so they can add a child's writing to the folder pocket whenever they wish. They may also provide paper in unusual shapes, word cards that offer the children models of writing, or a variety of writing implements to encourage journal writing. You can find out what kinds of journaling activities are done at your child's center and make similar journaling activities available at home. You might also encourage your child to write and draw pictures in her journal about activities she likes at preschool or child care. The teacher or provider might appreciate your help in making up folders for the children at the center. Or you could go to school and lead an activity in which all the children decorate the covers of folders that hold their journaling efforts.

Scrapbooks are an interesting variation on journals. They may include photographs, writing samples, artwork, and school artifacts, such as name tags and favorite class recipes. In their scrapbooks, children place photos, write down special memories, and record their friends' names, their favorite lunch, special books, familiar songs, favorite activities, and so on. The portfolios or more formal scrapbooks kept by teachers serve the additional purpose of documenting each child's development through the year. If your child's preschool or center is using scrapbooks, you can help your child choose photos from home to use in his book and, when you're at his school, you can look at his scrapbook with him.

Many centers document long-range group projects, special activities, or field trips. For instance, a preschool might have its children make a group movie, and the project might begin by recording the children's conversations as they talk about it. Boards could be made to display the children's writing about the conversations along with photos of the work in progress. The children might make a list of their ideas for the movie, lists of materials they need in order to make the movie, and so on. Children would be highly interested in such writing, since the content would reflect something they'd been involved in.

>Predictable Text

Besides supporting the emergence of reading, predictable text also can stimulate writing. The interactive charts we talked about in chapter 4 are one form of predictable text used in preschools and child care centers. In another form, children actually write words on the word cards instead of simply identifying or reading them, or they may complete predictable sentences on cards. You might help your child make greeting cards or holiday cards based on repeated text. You could, for example, write in a card, "I like you, _____," and your child could fill in her friend's name, and then sign her own name. Your child could then take the card to the center and put it in her friend's cubby.

>Story Starters

Young children can get very excited when an adult helps them weave a story about a favorite storybook character or offers them open-ended phrases for starting a story. For example, Shaquilla's grandma, who often read Curious George books to her, had noticed the story starters being used at Shaquilla's preschool. She decided to put a monkey sticker on a sheet of paper, and under it she printed, "One day Curious George . . ." She then wrote down the story Shaquilla made up about the little monkey. It was only two sentences long, but Shaquilla loved it. So Grandma Joanna made up enough sheets for all the children at preschool and Shaquilla shared her story with her classmates. Joanna might also have taken Shaquilla's completed story to the school and read it to the other children. Or she might have suggested that Shaquilla draw a picture using Curious George as a focal point and then make up a story about it.

>Building Writing Activities into the Environment

Preschools and child care centers often include writing materials as a part of all their play areas. Although small child care centers or family child care homes may not set up formal play areas, they still can integrate writing materials and activities into children's play throughout the day.

For example, if a dramatic play area is transformed

into a dance studio, writing tickets would be a logical outgrowth of play in that area. An observation notebook might be included in a science area, since careful observation is part of the scientific process. Children often want to write descriptions of the artwork they do. If children are playing restaurant, they can use pads of paper to write down orders or to create menus. One group of children designed in the block area of their classroom an amusement park, complete with signs labeling the various rides.

Try modifying such ideas at home. You can keep a small basket with paper and pencils near your child's play telephone, or keep a silverware caddy with paper, pencils, and markers on a shelf in your child's room or on a small table or desk in a play area. The play scenarios your child creates with his siblings or friends offer lots of opportunities for writing. Talk to the provider or teacher about things she's doing and replicate some of them at home. Observe what happens at the center and take those ideas home. As mentioned earlier, your child can help you write grocery lists or make place cards for family members. When your child is ready, he can write his own notes to his teacher or provider or to friends at the center. Or you can take his dictation, and your child can write (or scribble) his own name at the bottom of a note.

Some Sample Activities

Following we look at specific examples of writing exploration activities that are typical of those used in preschools and in some child care centers and family child care homes. Again, if your child's center doesn't use these activities, you could tell the center about them or even volunteer to develop some for the center. You also may wish to adapt them for home use.

> Pocket Stories

A pocket story is simply a young child's original artwork drawn on a piece of paper with a pocket at the bottom that holds a sentence or phrase about the art. To form a pocket, fold up and staple at the edges the bottom two inches of a nine-by-twelve-inch piece of paper. Then have your child draw or paint a picture on the paper and dictate a phrase or sentence about her drawing that you write on the outside of the pocket. To help your child get started, you can say, "Tell me about your picture, and I'll write the words you say on this pocket." Next, write on separate strips of paper each word of your child's phrase or sentence. Your child can then match the words to those in the phrase on the pocket and drop them into the pocket. She can also copy the words or, if she wishes, add other writing.

Children are often eager to match the individual words to the words written on the pocket. Some children will want to copy individual words to put into the pocket, and some will copy the entire phrase or sentence. Some older preschoolers or kindergarten-age children even create their own pocket stories. And some will notice punctuation and word placement. If your child is comfortable copying an entire sentence, you might want to suggest that she write the original sentence on the outside of the pocket.

To help your child think about the writing, you might ask, "Can you find the word on your pocket that matches this word?" Or, "Look at the word 'I.' It's a letter and a word." If your child is ready and interested in the sounds made by letters, you might say something such as, "Listen to the sound this word starts with. What letter do you think I need to write?" Or, "What sounds do you hear in this word?"

Ideas for Partnering with the Teacher or Provider

- Send your child's pocket story to preschool or child care and hang it in his cubby or have him share it at circle time.

- Make a blank pocket story that your child can take to the center. He can then draw on it there, and his teacher or provider can write his words on the pocket. If she does not have time for this, your child could bring the pocket story home for you to write the words.

- Make some blank pocket stories for your child to share with his friends at preschool or child care. Perhaps they can work side-by-side, something older preschoolers particularly enjoy.

- Suggest that your child draw a picture of something he does at the center or a picture of the center itself.

- Volunteer to help other children at the center make pocket stories.

- Volunteer to lead an activity at the center in which the children make a group pocket story. They might collaborate on a group mural and dictate a short story about it. You could then fold up a pocket at the bottom and create word cards for matching.

>Using Pictures as Story Starters

A rubber stamp or a sticker can serve as a story starter. A stamp, for example, might be of a favorite character from a book, or it might be an animal or a food or a shape such as a star. You can often find rubber stamps that match book characters at children's bookstores. You can also cut shapes from a sponge to make stamps. To begin, your child chooses a stamp and makes an impression with it on the top half of a piece of paper. Though not a requirement, it's helpful if the bottom of the paper is lined. Then, using pencils, markers, additional stamps, or any other material you want to provide, he completes his picture in any way he chooses. Finally, he either dictates or writes his own story to go with his picture.

Children who are just learning the relationship between spoken and written language will need to dictate their stories. In general, young children eagerly examine the words as they repeat what they've dictated. Some children want to add their own writing to what they've dictated. Others may want to copy what the adult has written. Children who write their own stories will use phonetic or standard spelling, depending on their stage of development.

If your child chooses to write his story, remember that this is not a time to correct spelling. He may, for example, place words in an order that looks strange to you, perhaps over or under each other, or spread out randomly. Accept his written words, no matter what they look like. You could, if you wish, write the words he's likely to use on cards ahead of time so he can see what the words look like and copy them.

When your child has completed his story, talk with him about it. You might ask questions such as, "What is Corduroy doing in your picture?" Or say, "Here's a word card for Strega Nona if you need to see how her name is spelled." To help your child notice phonemes, you could say, "You drew a picture of a mouse. What sound does 'mouse' start with?" Or, "This is interesting. 'Kitty' and 'cat' both start with the same sound, but a different letter represents the sound." Or, "You need the letters 's' and 'h' together to make that sound."

Ideas for Partnering with the Teacher or Provider

- Ask the teacher or provider if you can borrow a book that your child loves, and make a story starter at home using a character from that book.

- Borrow from the library a favorite book being used at the center, and make a story starter based on it at home.

- With your child, make sponge stamps about a book being used at preschool or child care and send the stamps to the center.

- Help your child make several story starters that he and the other children at child care can complete together.

>Family Day Cards

Many preschools and child care centers design activities that allow children to take messages home to their families. To make a family day card, the teacher or provider writes a phrase on the front of the card (made from a piece of colored paper folded in half) and inside, the child completes the phrase in her own writing. If, for example, a provider has been reading the books *I Love My Mommy Because . . .* and *I Love My Daddy Because . . .* to the children, she could write on the outside of a card, "I love my mommy because," and inside a child might dictate her answer for the provider to write, such as, "she takes me to the park."

Providers at preschools and child care centers are usually careful to shift a card to read "I love my grandma . . ." or "I love my aunt . . ." or "I love my uncle . . ." when a child has a guardian other than her mother or father. If this is the case in your family, make sure the teacher or provider is making appropriate adjustments.

These types of cards can be made at home as well. You might write, "I love my grandma (or another special person) because . . ." on the outside of the card. You could also make cards on the computer, remembering to use a standard font such as Arial. Then ask your child to scribble-write (most children won't be ready to write whole sentences accurately until age six and older) her message on the inside of the card. Younger children may need to dictate the message to you, or you may need to write part of the message and they can add a word, a letter, or scribblings.

Young children are generally eager to write their sentiments on cards, and some want to create cards for numerous family members. You can help your child think about the writing by asking questions such as, "Can you find the card that says 'grandpa'?" You can encourage phonetic awareness through statements such as, "I hear lots of 'd' sounds in 'daddy.' Look at all the 'd's.'" Or, "'Y' can sound like 'ee' at the end of a word. Look at the end of 'daddy.'"

Ideas for Partnering with the Teacher or Provider

- Make cards for the teacher, provider, other children in the preschool or child care, the janitor, the cook, or other staff.

- Send to school or child care any sample greeting cards/envelopes you receive in the mail so the children can use them.

- Ask your child regularly whether anyone was sick or absent from school. Then make together a "miss you" card for that person.

- Some centers or family child care homes encourage children to bring cards to school on special occasions, such as Halloween or Valentine's Day. You can help your child make cards for these occasions. Be sure to make a card for every child.

• • •

Summary of Partnering Ideas

- Ask your child's teacher or provider about the writing exploration activities she's using at the center.

- Keep writing materials handy around the house, perhaps in a basket or a silverware caddy.

- Write down your child's stories, notes, or messages and take them or send them to the center.

- Read to your child any notes sent home by the teacher, provider, or friends.

- Help your child keep a journal or scrapbook at home that includes stories, photos, and special items from preschool or child care. Share the journal or scrapbook with your child's teacher or provider.

- Offer to make journals or scrapbooks for the children at the center.

- Help your child write (by dictation or scribble-writing if necessary) a sentence about the artwork he brings home from school.

- Have your child take blank cards or pocket story sheets to the center.

- Volunteer to make with the children at the center a poster about a field trip they've taken.

- Help your child write to grandma or grandpa a letter about his preschool or child care center.

Chapter 8
Writing Spaces

Larry and Kamal were best friends at Oak Hill Child Care Center. They were almost five years old and would be starting kindergarten in a few months. One day, when they asked their teacher if they could sit next to each other at lunch, she suggested they write her a reminder message. After rushing to the writing center and picking up pencils from the tray, they looked at their teacher questioningly. Knowing both boys could write their names, she told them to pick out one piece of paper and write their names on it. When they'd finished, she asked them if they knew how to write the word "lunch." When they shook their heads, she wrote the word for them in large letters on a card and asked them to copy it onto the paper where they'd written their names. (She might also have said "lunch" several times, emphasizing the "l" sound, to see if the boys could figure out which letter the word began with.) "Hey, that letter is in my name," said Larry, pointing at the "l." "You're exactly right," said the teacher. "Can you find that letter in Kamal's name too?"

The writing center at Oak Hill made it easy for children to respond to the teacher's suggestion and for the teacher to continue to encourage writing. Many preschools and child care centers create these special spaces for writing.

A writing center generally is a child-sized table with writing materials in a special area of the room that encourages young children to experiment with handwriting and creative writing. Writing centers may be organized around themes, books, or activities that are especially interesting to children, and a preschool or child care center may rotate different focuses through its writing center throughout the year.

How Writing Centers Help Children Learn

As young children make the transition into writing, they need an environment that encourages them to express themselves, easy access to paper and writing tools, and a convenient space for experimenting with writing. Having a writing center at hand makes it easy for a child to explore this skill anytime. With its neatly arranged, interesting materials, the center itself makes writing appealing. And because a center usually has space for two or three, children can offer their ideas and both help and inspire each other.

Word cards, which give young children the opportunity to copy meaningful print, are often available in writing centers. The cards provide models of conventional print and motivate children to try to approximate the letters. Children especially enjoy copying their names and the names of others. All such explorations build a foundation for success in written communication.

How to Be a Partner with the Provider or Teacher in Using Writing Centers

A basic writing center typically has plenty of space for writing at the table and is located against a wall or peg board or the back of a shelf so that children's writing samples, as well as labels, signs, and other printed materials, can be displayed. It also is likely to have a variety of colored paper and pencils, plus desk or drawer organizers for holding supplies so they're easy to find and the table doesn't get cluttered. Teachers and providers also may include word cards, a movable alphabet, alphabet rubber stamps, high-interest books, or a model of the alphabet. Although, because of space constraints, a family child care home is less apt to have a permanent writing center, it may have some version of one, if only a small table on which writing materials and paper are made available on a regular basis.

Young, inexperienced children may need only a simple arrangement of paper, pencils, and name cards, while children who are older and more experienced can make use of more extensive writing supplies. It's important that a writing table not become so crowded with materials that it's distracting. Also, art materials, such as glue, scissors, and tape, should not be included in a writing center. Such items are apt to distract children from experimenting with writing.

To help children remain interested, teachers and providers often change the materials in a writing center every two or three weeks. Even a new batch of pencils with different decorations can be interesting to children.

The color of the paper might be changed to reflect seasonal changes, and word cards might be changed to reflect what's happening in the classroom or center.

If your child's preschool or care setting has no writing center, you might talk with the teacher or provider to see if she's interested in establishing one. She may prefer to work with the children in other ways, or she simply may have no time to set one up. If you have the time to help her, she may welcome your assistance.

If your child is in a family child care setting that has no space for a writing center, your provider might appreciate having a movable one. Mike, whose daughter was in family child care, bought a writing tray that was designed to be used in bed. It was a plastic box with a soft bottom and a hard top that opened. Mike filled the box with pieces of paper cut in interesting shapes, a couple of pencils decorated with storybook characters, and a batch of colored markers. Soon after he gave it to his daughter's provider, she told him the children often asked to use it. One of them, she said, would find a cozy corner, sit on the floor, and happily play with the writing-center-in-a-box for long periods of time.

You may want to make a writing center for use at home, perhaps in a child's room or in a play area. If you don't have space for a chair and table, you can get a little storage box with divisions in it and rotate its materials. Remember that your writing center should focus on a topic that interests your child. Then the words he's writing will be words that he cares about, words that communicate things that matter to him.

If your child attends a preschool or child care program that has a writing center, pay attention to what's being done there so you can add curriculum-related words to your writing center. You could print the names of your child's friends at preschool or child care on cards for your writing center. You could also make word cards at home and send them to the preschool or center in a folder so your child can continue his efforts from home at preschool or child care.

Children use a writing center in a variety of ways. Even very young children are generally familiar with paper and pencils and will immediately begin to make marks or produce some form of personal print when they have access to a writing center. Children with more experience or a strong interest in writing will probably copy word cards and write messages. In the beginning, your child may be more interested in reading the name cards than in making marks on paper. If she resists using the writing materials at all, don't force the issue. Let her take up writing activities at her own pace.

Sample Activities

Described below and on the following pages are three examples of writing centers you can set up in your home.

>Alphabet Writing Center

This writing center focuses on children's interest in the alphabet book *Chicka Chicka Boom Boom*. An activity described in chapter 4 also was based on this rhythmic alphabet book.

To set up this writing center, start with containers for

holding pencils, paper, word cards, and name cards printed with your child's name and with the names of friends,
family members, or other children at preschool or child
care. You may want to add rubber alphabet stamps for
both upper- and lowercase letters. It's helpful to have a
copy of *Chicka Chicka Boom Boom* at the table and to use
brightly colored construction paper to match the book.

You can get your child started by asking him to find
his name among the name cards and to print it using the
rubber stamps. Depending on his age, he may just want
to experiment with the rubber stamps without copying
his name, or he may be interested and experienced
enough to copy his name using a pencil. You can also
show him how to use name cards to write messages.
Depending on your child's developmental level, you may
wish to limit your selection of alphabet stamps to uppercase letters.

While playing with your child at his writing center,
you can ask questions and make comments such as "Can
you find a stamp for the first letter in your name?" "Use
the capital letter (this one) for the first letter in your
name." "Let's say each sound as you stamp your name."

Ideas for Partnering with the Teacher or Provider

- Ask your child's teacher or provider for a list of the names
  of the other children so you can make name cards for your
  writing center.
- Help your child write notes to his friends and then have
  him take what he's written to his preschool or center.
- With your help, your child may wish to use the letter

stamps to make simple bingo boards for a family game. (You can read more about this game in chapter 10.)

• Create a simple picture of a coconut tree. As you read *Chicka Chicka Boom Boom* to your child, he can stamp the appropriate letters onto the tree. He can take this tree to preschool or child care to share at circle time.

>Construction Zone Writing Center

Many young children enjoy pretending to fix things, and many early childhood programs include woodworking activities. In addition to basic writing materials, this writing center includes word cards for tools such as a hammer, saw, screwdriver, or pliers. You might also include stickers or illustrations of the tools named on the word cards as well as half and quarter sheets of red, yellow, green, orange, and white paper. Once again, include name cards.

As your child plays at this writing center, you might ask her which play tools she has in her room, or which tools you have in your home. Ask her to help you find the word card for a particular tool. You might also add word cards for such construction vehicles as a backhoe, front loader, dump truck, or crane. Ask your child what sound she hears at the beginning of words such as "hammer."

Ideas for Partnering with the Teacher or Provider

• Visit your child's preschool or care center to see what play tools or construction vehicles they have, and make matching word cards.

- Send your child's writing samples to school or the center to be shared with the teacher or provider and the other children.
- Make construction and tool word cards that your child's preschool, care center, or family care home can use in a writing center.
- Volunteer to assist children at your child's preschool or child care with a woodworking activity. It could be as simple as pounding nails into a log. Be sure that both you and the children wear safety goggles. Afterward, the children can write about their experience.
- Create some small construction zone journals your child can share with classmates. Simply cut paper in the shape of a tool, such as a saw, and staple several sheets together. The children can write in their individual "tool books."

>Grocery Store Writing Center

This writing center fits easily into home, child care, or preschool settings. Most young children are accustomed to going to the grocery store with a parent from time to time. They love choosing their own cereal or snacks or yogurt. Most preschools and child care centers have dramatic play areas centered around food in one way or another, and the props from such an area can be used to set up a grocery store.

For this writing center, you can make word cards of grocery items such as cereal, milk, soap, macaroni and cheese, banana, apple, orange, and so on. Again, stickers or illustrations can be used as cues to the meaning of words. You can add more word cards if your child is older and more experienced. You could also include a notepad for making shopping lists, as well as box fronts or labels from cans. You might even add tracing paper so your child could trace the labels.

You can ask your child what he wants to write on his shopping list, or ask him to help you find the word card for "apple." If you notice that your child has used the notepad, you might say, "This paper is full of writing. Help me read what you wrote." You can encourage phonetic awareness with comments such as, "Listen to the beginning of 'cereal.' This time the 's' sound is made by a 'c.'" Or, "What sound does 'apple' start with? An 'a' makes that sound."

Ideas for Partnering with the Teacher or Provider

- Visit your child's preschool or care center to see what food or grocery store props are being used, and make matching word cards for home.

- After getting the teacher or provider's approval, let your child help you pick out box fronts or can labels to send to the preschool or child care center.

- Visit the library with your child and select some books about foods or grocery stores. Share them with your child's class or child care center.

• • •

Summary of Partnering Ideas

- Talk with the teacher or provider to see if she's using writing centers.

- Offer to help set up a permanent writing center or to make a movable one.
- Make word cards for a home writing center that echo preschool or child care activities and curriculum.
- Get a list of the other children's names from the teacher or provider so you can make name cards for them in your writing center at home.
- Make with your child word cards to give to her preschool or child care.

Chapter 9
Traveling Words

Preschools and child care centers sometimes use what are called literacy suitcases. These small plastic cases or even backpacks generally contain a selected child's book and related writing materials. Young children usually become very excited about taking such a suitcase home for a short period of time, which in turn promotes their interest in writing. Literacy suitcases are a natural choice for strengthening the connection between home and school and allowing you to have an active partnership with the teacher or provider.

How Literacy Suitcases Help Children Learn

As essentially another version of a writing center, literary suitcases encourage the same skills and concepts as a writing center does. In addition, they help you get ideas from the teacher or provider on ways to encourage writing, they help you get information on literacy development, and they let the teacher or provider know what you're doing at home.

Literacy suitcases make excellent travel companions. The books and writing materials they contain keep children productively occupied while waiting in the doctor's office, traveling to and from child care, waiting for older siblings to finish their activities, or going on a trip.

How to Be a Partner with the Provider or Teacher in Using Literacy Suitcases

A literacy suitcase generally holds a book, a variety of sizes and types of paper, a couple of pencils, name cards for the children in the class or center, and an alphabet sample. It also includes a note to parents from the teacher or provider and a note to the child about how to use the case and when to return it. The child, of course, depends on a parent to read the notes. The container itself could be a small plastic case, a small lunch box, an empty craft box, a backpack, or even an old briefcase.

Supplemental materials in a literacy suitcase might include extra word cards, some markers, or some envelopes. The word cards should have stickers or illustrations as cues to help the child recognize the words. Predictable books are especially valuable in a literacy suitcase because word cards can be made to go with the book. An example of such a book is *Dear Zoo* by Rod Campbell, which contains a predictable sentence and focuses on zoo animals. Children typically are very interested in the story and enjoy reading the names of the animals on word cards and attempting to copy the words.

Teachers or providers sometimes add to suitcases blank books or fill-in-the-blank papers, which are pieces of paper with phrases that can be completed by a child in various ways. As with writing centers, literacy suitcases should not include art supplies, which encourage children to focus on art activities rather than on writing explorations.

Literacy suitcases require so little space that they can easily be used in every kind of child care setting. If your child's teacher or provider doesn't use this fun tool, you might offer to make her one. First, however, be sure she understands how a suitcase works and that she has the time to integrate using one into her program.

If your child's teacher or provider already uses literacy suitcases, you might ask her which suitcase supplies would be useful, and send them to school with your child. You could also take photos of the children at the center (with permission, of course) and mount them on name cards for the school's suitcases. Picture cards with symbols for sign language can be included for children who communicate using signs. A tape recording of a book might be included for a non-English-speaking child.

When your child brings home a literacy suitcase, take the time to open it with him, go through the contents, and sit with him while he uses it. Ask him about the word cards and, if he's interested, point out various letters and sounds. Read with him any book included in the suitcase. Remember to accept all of his writing, whether or not it's grammatical or has spelling errors. At this point, you merely want to encourage his interest in exploring writing.

Taylor's mom, Cleo, made a literacy suitcase to take along on the family's trip to Yellowstone National Park. She hoped it would help to occupy her kids during the eight hours they'd have to spend in the car. First Cleo borrowed from the library a book that was being used in Taylor's preschool. She tucked the book, which was about bears, into a plastic container, to which she added a notebook, some colored sheets of paper, markers, and stickers of bears.

Making that suitcase turned out to be one of the best ideas Cleo ever had. Taylor, who was four years old, drew endless pictures of bears in the notebook and "signed" her name, a large "T" followed by scribbles, on every page. Taylor, her dad and mom, and her eight-year-old brother made up lots of stories about bears, taking turns adding to the stories. Cleo wrote some of the stories in the notebook as the family spun them. After naptime, Taylor was eager to pull out the literacy suitcase again, and often her big brother would write words in the notebook for her. When Taylor returned to school, she brought her literacy suitcase, along with photographs, so she could share some of her trip adventures with her teacher and classmates.

Literacy suitcases are easy to travel with, in a car or on an airplane. They can also be invaluable in occupying your child in a setting where he has to be patient and quiet. If you're making a literacy suitcase for traveling, you could, like Cleo, base it on a book being used at your child's preschool or child care center and include in it the names of the other children. Your child could then take the suitcase to school when you're back from your trip.

Sample Activities

Three examples of literacy suitcases are described below and on the following pages.

›Post Office Literacy Suitcase

This literacy suitcase calls for various colors of paper, some lined paper, and envelopes of different sizes and colors. It should also include an alphabet sample and a pen or pencils. If you're making the suitcase for home or for a family trip, you could include in an inexpensive address book the names and addresses of friends and relatives. You also might include the names and addresses of the teachers or providers and, with parental permission, the names and addresses of the other children in the class or child care. Including a few pieces of junk mail in the suitcase might make it feel more grown-up or real to your child.

You might add actual stationery, or add stickers so your child could make his own. At the top of the stationery, you could write "Dear _____," and your child could copy in the space the names of friends, family, or classmates (either first name, or first and last name). If your child is a more experienced writer, he might add some words to a message or even be able to copy an address on the envelope. Or he may just add scribblings or marks to the paper, and perhaps copy his name at the bottom of the sheet. You could also offer to take dictation, and your child could add his name at the bottom. You might walk with your child to the post office, buy stamps, and mail his messages.

Ideas for Partnering with the Teacher or Provider

- Include in your suitcase the names and addresses of teachers, providers, or children at the school.

- Mail your child's notes to the teacher, provider, or friends.

- If the teacher or caregiver likes the idea of having a mailbox for each child, you might volunteer to make small mailboxes out of milk cartons or shoe boxes.

- Save junk mail envelopes and advertising stickers, such as those from record or book clubs, for use at preschool or child care. When playing post office, children quickly go through many envelopes and stamps.

- Help your child send away for free things. She'll both get to write her name and see her name in print when she gets mail. Your library may have a book for children about where to send for free things.

> Apple Literacy Suitcase

This literacy suitcase can be coordinated with many activities in the autumn. If your family goes apple picking, or goes to a farmers' market to buy apples, or picks apples from the tree in your yard, your child is likely to be highly interested in this suitcase. You could also take your child to the grocery store to buy apples and then make applesauce or apple pie.

You can use quarter sheets of yellow, green, and red paper to echo the colors of various apples. You might also include a pencil decorated with an apple, or a red pencil decorated with apple stickers. The word cards should include "red," "green," "yellow," and "apple," along with your child's and others' names. You could write the words for colors in the color identified. You could also include apple-shaped paper or fill-in-the-blank paper that reads, "I like apples best." Don't forget the alphabet sample.

Your child may copy the color words, along with the word "apple." He may copy only one letter of a word, or he may carefully study a word card and then pretend to duplicate it. If you're making applesauce or apple pie, you might also include in your suitcase an index card with the recipe written on it. Your child might want to help you make a list of the groceries you need to buy for the sauce or pie. As with all our reading and writing explorations, you can comment on the letters and sounds in the words, or ask your child, for instance, to find the card that contains the word "red."

Ideas for Partnering with the Teacher or Provider

- Find out if your child's teacher or care provider is doing any special activities organized around apples in the autumn, and make word cards that coordinate with those activities.

- Along with your child's writing about apples, send apples to the teacher or provider and to the other children.

- Cut out pieces of apple-shaped paper for your child to share with the children at school or child care.
- Make an apple literacy suitcase for your child's preschool or his care center or home.

> Sleepy-Animals Literacy Suitcase

This suitcase coordinates with a poetry book by Mem Fox titled *Time for Bed,* whose poems describe the bedtime routines of various animal families. Besides a copy of the book, your suitcase should contain a word card for each animal in the book with an illustration of that animal. You might also add paper cutouts of some of the animals. Quarter sheets of pastel paper go well with this book, and, for a change of pace, you might add several thin markers. Include, as before, a card with your child's name and cards with the names of friends, family members, and so on, as well as an alphabet model.

Your child may copy the animal words on the pieces of paper. She also may draw the animals. If you include a thin blank book, your child may make up an animal story of her own. You'll probably have to take dictation for most of the story, but she may wish to copy in the animal words or names that she wants to include. Or she may wish to add her marks or scribblings to the dictation you've written down. Remember to write her words exactly as she says them, even if her grammar is improper. As mentioned earlier, if you correct her verbal story as you write, she'll have difficulty connecting her spoken words with what you've written. Over time, with your modeling, correct grammar will come.

Ideas for Partnering with the Teacher or Provider

- If your child's teacher or provider doesn't have *Time for Bed*, lend it to her or buy her a copy.

- Share your literacy suitcase with the teacher or provider.

- If your child makes up his own story, send it to preschool with him, along with a note to the teacher asking her to read it.

- This book is perfect for naptime. If the children at preschool or child care take naps, record the story with soft music playing in the background and send the tape recorder with your child. She and all the children can listen to it as they rest.

> Other Literacy Suitcases

Literacy suitcases can be built around other children's books and around many themes. Ideas include summer, autumn, winter, or spring; holidays; farm animals and activities; and cooking and food.

• • •

Summary of Partnering Ideas

- Talk with the teacher or provider about whether she uses literacy suitcases.

- If she doesn't, ask if she'd like you to make one that can be rotated among the children.

- If your child's preschool, center, or home uses literacy suitcases, send back extra material when you return a suitcase. Ask the teacher or provider what materials she needs.

- When your child brings home a literacy suitcase, sit with him and go through the materials, read the book and talk with him about it, and encourage and notice his writing.
- Remember to accept all of your child's writing as it is.

Chapter 10
Fun and Games with Words

Games have probably been around as long as there've been people to play them. One story from Chinese history tells us that Emperor Shun, who was born in 2255 B.C., invented a strategy game called Wei Ch'i to help develop the intelligence of his son. Games provide a reason to gather, a way to interact and have fun, and a way to learn, to keep our minds active and inquiring. If as a parent you both enjoy playing games with your children and recognize that playing them also encourages learning, you're part of a long tradition.

Many preschools, child care centers, and homes capitalize on young children's pleasure in games and what are called manipulative materials to encourage both reading and writing skills. Manipulative materials include any item that can be handled and moved around and is used for learning. Examples are the puzzle pieces children use to learn the names of states or alphabet letters, beads and blocks when they're used to learn math, and plastic or magnetic alphabet letters.

Children generally are eager to play with manipulative materials and games, making them an easy, fun tool to use in encouraging literacy skills both at school and at home.

How Games and Manipulative Materials Help Children Learn

As young children play with literacy games and manipulative materials, they become familiar with letter shapes and forms. They learn to distinguish letters from other symbols and begin to identify specific letters. They apply the ideas of same, different, and similar to letters, and they begin to form letter–word and letter–sound relationships.

Letter games or alphabet bingo help children recognize that letters are a group of symbols. Word games help them construct the relationship between letters and words. Movable alphabets encourage word play, which also helps children understand letter–word relationships. They learn that not every combination of letters results in a word, and that it takes a specific set and sequence of letters to make a specific word. Materials such as flannelboard pieces or puppets or small lifelike figures allow children to continue playing out a story, which helps them with reading comprehension skills such as recognizing characters and story sequences (beginning, middle, end).

How to Be a Partner with the Provider or Teacher in Using Games and Manipulative Materials

To spur children's interest in and comfort level with

written language, teachers and providers often use letter and word games and physical representations of letters and other things children can handle. A teacher might, for instance, include a magnetic or movable alphabet to play with. (If you're using a movable alphabet at home, be sure to keep letters arranged in a way that makes it easy for your child to locate the letters she's looking for. Divided trays, sewing or tackle boxes with drawers, and holders with pockets are useful for organizing movable alphabets.) A teacher or provider might offer sponge letters as printing tools with paint, letter molds to use with playdough, or foam letters for adhering to flat surfaces or for play in a water table. (In such a table, children play with water and various vessels and utensils as they improve their small motor skills and are exposed to such things as the concepts of weight and volume.)

These kinds of materials are widely available in toy stores and are easy and fun to use at home. If you prefer, you can make them yourself. You can cut story characters from felt for a flannelboard, or cut letters from cardboard and color them. You can use stuffed animals to dramatize a story, or make puppets out of old stuffed socks.

If you're making games, be sure to print clearly and accurately. Young children have trouble recognizing letters that are crooked or formed incorrectly. Put clear self-adhesive plastic coating on game pieces so they stand up to children's play. Add illustrations to word games to support recognition.

You might ask your child's teacher or provider which games and manipulative materials she's using with your child so you can use the same or similar ones at home. This will reinforce what your child is learning at preschool or child care. If you're making games or manipulative materials, you might ask the teacher or provider if she'd like some for her program. You and your child could work on them together.

Many of the materials we're talking about can be picked up inexpensively at secondhand stores or yard sales. You can probably find foam letters at a dollar store, and your child can play with them in the bathtub. After you've wet the walls lightly so foam will stick, your shower also can be used as a play area. Some foam letters also will stick to sliding glass doors on a patio. The teacher or provider may have additional simple ideas for using hands-on materials.

You might ask the teacher or provider if your child could bring home a game overnight or for the weekend, or if you could send one of your child's favorite games to preschool or child care. Remember, however, that pieces get lost easily, and teachers and providers may not have time for close monitoring.

Preschools and child care centers often appreciate having parents make take-home games, such as bingo, for all the children. Parents could even get together outside of school hours and make materials the teacher needs.

Sample Activities

The following literacy games are easy to make and easy and fun to play.

★ Alphabet Activities

- Draw letters in soap bubbles in the bathtub.
- Draw letters in sand at the park.
- Help your child write her name in the sand.
- Use spray foam to write letters in the bath or shower.
- Put foam letters on the wet wall of the shower or on sliding glass doors.
- Put magnetic letters on the refrigerator door. Spell your child's name.
- Using letter blocks, build your child's name and other recognizable words.

＞Word Bank Game

This game is for children who are starting to recognize words and are showing an interest in reading, which usually doesn't happen until age five or older. First make a word bank with your child. Clearly print your words on three-by-five-inch index cards. Because children seem to learn to read first the words they find interesting, you might use your child's name, the word "dog" if he has one, the name of his favorite storybook character, his favorite food, and so on. Involve your child in deciding what words he wants in his word bank. Add maybe just one new word each day. When too many words are added at once, children can't remember them. Keep the word cards in a small box such as a recipe box, or you could punch a hole in the top of each card and hang them all on a hook labeled, for example, "Maya's Word Bank."

Once your child has ten words in her word bank, write the words on cutout paper stars (or another shape your child finds especially interesting—clouds, perhaps, or cats or trucks). To play the game, have your child place the stars face down and turn them over one at a time. She gets a point for each word she reads correctly. You can keep a tally for each time you go through the bank so your child is challenged to better her last record. If, on a particular day, your child is having trouble remembering words and is becoming discouraged, put the game away until a time when she wants to play it. If she isn't having fun, it's not a game—it's not *play*—and she won't associate her early reading experiences with pleasure.

Because the words are of high interest to him, your child tends to remember the words printed on his word bank cards. Once you've written those same words on cards of a different shape, he may at first have difficulty reading them, because they're in a context different from the word bank. If this is true for your child, you can make comments and ask questions such as "You turned over a word that starts with 'm.' Can you help me read it?" Or "I see the word 'fire' on both of these stars—'fire truck' and 'firefighter.'" "You read this word as 'Dan,' and that's almost what it says. Look at the last letter. How would that 'd' sound at the end of the word?"

This game can encourage your child to add new words to his word bank. You can tell him that when he has twenty words in his word bank, he can have another game with words written on another shape he likes. You can also offer him movable alphabet letters so he can form the words in his word bank.

Ideas for Partnering Games with the Teacher or Provider

- If your child's teacher or provider is using word banks, find out which words your child has in her bank.

- Help your child make word cards for both his home and school word banks.

- Volunteer to cut out the shapes being used for this game at school.

★Lucky Star Game

The star-shaped cards for this game bear words that are important to your child. To play, your child turns all the star cards face down and then picks out a card one at a time and reads the word on it. If she reads the word correctly, she gets a point. Play continues until she's read all the cards.

>Letter Memory Game

You're probably familiar with the many versions of memory games available in children's toy stores. These games have small cards with pictures of objects. Each card has one duplicate. To play the game, all the cards are turned face down, and the child and another person take turns turning two cards face up to find matching pairs. When the child makes a match, she keeps the pair. If she fails to make a match, the cards are turned face down and the other person takes a turn.

To make this same game at home, print the entire alphabet on index cards twice, one letter per card. Make sure the cards are all the same color so your child doesn't try to use colors for matching cards. For younger children, start with capital letters, which are easier to distinguish than lowercase letters. If your child is beginning to recognize words, you can use the cards in his word bank to play this game.

Matching cards entices children to look carefully at letters or words. You can help your child think about letters or words by making comments such as, "These two words almost match, but look at the last letter. 'Car' ends with an 'r' and 'cat' ends with a 't.'" Or, for the word "bee," "Look at the first letter. It makes a 'buh' sound. The two 'e's together make this sound—'ee.'"

Ideas for Partnering with the Teacher or Provider

- Invite a friend from preschool or child care to your house to play the letter memory game with your child.
- Ask if your child can bring her letter memory game to preschool or child care.
- Volunteer to play this game with other children at your child's preschool or child care.

> Alphabet Bingo

This version of bingo, the ever-popular game, is easy to make. You play it by holding up a letter card and asking your child to look for that letter on his board. If he finds it, he covers it with a bottle cap, a penny, or another type of marker. This game encourages your child to look carefully at how each letter is made.

You can make bingo sheets with seven-by-six-inch pieces of white poster board. Divide each sheet into twelve squares and print a different letter in each square. Make several of the sheets so that you use all the alphabet letters in varying combinations. Having a number of sheets also allows friends or family members to play the game with your child. Print the alphabet letters on individual index cards that you can hold up for matching. Again, you can start with capital letters and switch to lowercase letters once your child becomes familiar with capitals.

As you play the game, name each letter aloud, or ask your child to name the letter you're holding up. When she finds it on her board, you can also ask your child what sound that letter makes.

Ideas for Partnering with the Teacher or Provider

- Invite a friend from preschool or child care to your house to play the game with your child.
- Ask if your child can bring his alphabet bingo game to preschool or child care.
- Make multiple bingo sheets for your child's teacher or provider to use at school.

⟩ Grab Bag

For this game, wooden, plastic, or magnetic letters are placed in a small bag. Each player has a game board with several words printed on it. As the bag is passed around, players take turns drawing out of it one letter at a time.

They then try to match the letter to one of the letters on their board. If the letter a player draws doesn't match any letter on her board, she returns the letter to the bag. Play continues until all the words have been spelled.

You can make the game boards with six-by-eight-inch pieces of white poster board. Using a dark pen or marker, write words on the game boards by tracing around the letters from the set that will be in the grab bag. It's a good idea to laminate the boards or cover them with clear self-adhesive paper. Stickers or illustrations also add interest for children.

This game can help a child gain a much better understanding of how letters go together to form words. Of course, if your child is young and inexperienced with letters and words, you'll want to use short, easy ones.

As you play, you can ask your child if he can find a place on his board where the letter he's chosen will fit. You can ask what letter he needs to find in the bag in order to finish a word. You can also encourage phonetic awareness by telling your child, for instance, to listen to the sound "a" makes in the word "cat" on his board, or ask what sound "duck" starts with.

Ideas for Partnering with the Teacher or Provider

- Find out what words are being read at school and which words your child in particular is able to read. Use these words on your game boards.

- Invite a classmate or friend from child care to your house to play the game with your child.

- Ask if your child can bring her grab bag game to preschool or child care.

- Make game boards for your child's teacher or provider to use at school.

• • •

Summary of Partnering Ideas

- Talk with the teacher or provider to find out how she's using literacy games and manipulative materials.

- Buy or make similar materials to use at home.

- Find out which letters or words your child recognizes so you can use them in games at home.

- If possible, borrow from his preschool or child care games your child especially likes.

- Send from home to preschool or child care games your child especially likes.
- Volunteer to lead literacy games at preschool or child care.

Afterword

Read her a book. Write her a note. Sing him a song. Put a name on his tote. From Dr. Seuss to rap music, children love the clever use of words. And luckily, rhyming and alliteration and other word play is fun for young children and adults alike.

We can't say it too many times: play is learning and learning is play. Young children learn the skills that go into early reading and writing as part of their everyday lives, as part of their play, in all the environments young children occupy, from home to large child care centers, from family child care homes to preschools. All the adults they meet are teachers in one way or another, which means that parents and preschool teachers and providers are all partners in a young child's education.

• • •

Points to Remember

- Young children learn to read and write by seeing and using words in the context of their normal activities. Words must have meaning for children to care about and understand them. A child cares a lot more about seeing the word "Open" when she knows it means she can play in the park.

- Young children learn from the whole to the part, not the other way around. "J" makes no sense by itself. But "J" makes a lot of sense to Jim once he knows it's part of his name. Children can't take individual pieces of a puzzle and put them together until they see the whole picture. They have to see the whole picture first, and then the individual pieces start to make sense.

- Young children learn in predictable sequences. This is true for both reading and writing. Children learn to recognize that print has meaning before they recognize that print can be broken down into words. They scribble before they form letters.

- Young children learn best with lots of affirmation and acceptance.

- Young children learn at different rates. Although children follow similar patterns, each child learns at her own pace. Pushing a child too fast hurts rather than helps her learning.

As we've emphasized throughout this book, young children's learning is enhanced when parents can form partnerships with preschool teachers and child care providers. We've talked a lot about what you can do to foster such a partnership. On the next page we offer a summary checklist of those suggestions that you can copy and tape up for quick reference.

Partnering Checklist

___ Have conversations about books your child is reading at preschool or child care.

___ Read the same or similar books at home.

___ Lend favorite books to the teacher or provider.

___ Ask the provider which books are getting special attention at school, and have props at home for playing out those stories.

___ Read aloud the notes and information your child brings home from child care.

___ Draw attention to words and letters in your child's environment.

___ On a manila file folder, re-create illustrations of favorite book characters. Then cut them out and attach them to popsicle sticks to create puppets.

___ Read your child's name on his cubby.

___ Place your child's name over his coat hook at home.

___ Look at the labels used at preschool or child care and make similar labels at home. Print large, clear labels for toys shelves, bookshelves, or your child's bedroom door, and add picture cues so she can recognize the words.

___ Leave notes in your child's cubby that the teacher or provider can read to him after you leave.

___ Write your child's thoughts or words in a diary that she can take along to child care, where the provider can do the same. Pass the diary back and forth.

___ Use magnetic alphabet letters or words for the refrigerator door, and make words that your child is making at preschool or child care.

___ At home, make interactive charts, such as job charts, that incorporate activities your child does at school.

___ Make interactive charts that the teacher or provider can use.

___ In large, clear print, write menus for preschool or child care lunches that can be shared with all the children.

___ Send a snack with your child and attach a label with the name of the snack written in large, clear letters.

___ Help your child choose empty food containers for the dramatic play areas at preschool or child care.

___ Help your child write and mail notes to the other children at preschool or child care. Take her dictation. Let her sign her name, even if her signature is simply a scribble.

___ Make a literacy suitcase for your child's preschool or child care so children can take turns carrying it home.

___ Go on a field trip and help the children make a poster about what they did on the trip.

___ Help your child create a telephone and address book that includes the names of children in his preschool or child care.

___ Send to preschool or child care a story your child wrote on a family trip.

___ Play a simple game such as alphabet bingo with your child.

___ Invite other children home to play the game with your child.

___ Send the game to preschool or child care.

Appendix
Choosing Quality Child Care

Because profound growth and change occur during the first five years of a child's life, the child care experience you choose can play a significant role in your child's physical, social, emotional, and cognitive development. The child care field has responded to increased awareness of the importance of early learning and development by offering families a variety of quality care options.

Setting Goals That Meet Your Child's Needs

As you go about choosing child care, keep in mind the goals and values that are uniquely important to your family. Remember that what may be an ideal care arrangement for a neighbor or a coworker may not be what works well for your child or family. If it's important to you that siblings who need care have plenty of time together, you'll probably want to look for a licensed home or a center where children are in mixed-age groups. If, on the other hand, you believe your child would benefit from a larger group experience with the opportunity to interact with a variety of children and adults, you might want to look at child care centers.

Just as there are many different parenting styles, quality child care comes in many different models. It's important that you choose a model and setting that both supports your family values and goals and meets the quality standards you decide are essential for your child. Rates vary by type of program, qualifications of staff, adult-child ratios, and demographics, and better programs often cost more. If a program you like is priced outside your budget, look into funding assistance options such as the child care tax credit and dependent-care flex spending accounts.

Before choosing a child care setting, take the time to carefully consider your answers to these questions:

- What is my child like? What personality traits have emerged?

- What are my child's special needs now? What possible future needs might my child have?

- What are my child's interests? Have any special skills become apparent?

- What are my family's practical needs—schedule, budget, and so on?

- What values and traditions—religious and cultural ones, for instance—are important to my family?

- What goals do I have for my child? Do I want my child to:

    >learn how to play well with others?

    >be more independent and confident?

>be prepared for school?

>have a fun, safe experience?

Child Care Options

Although there are a variety of child care models—some based on a specific philosophy or approach, such as Montessori or Reggio, and others with a religious or cultural focus—there are three basic settings in which child care is delivered.

- In-Home Care. The caregiver, who may be a family member, a friend, or a professional provider, comes into your home.
- Family Child Care. The caregiver provides care for your child and other children, usually of various ages, in his or her home. Family child care providers should be licensed or registered by your state or county agency.
- School-Based or Independent Child Care Centers. Your child is cared for by a staff—usually one trained in early childhood education—in a regulated setting that often has educationally designed play areas and a schedule of programmed activities for children grouped by age.

To find out about programs available in your area, look up your regional Child Care Resource and Referral Agency. Because they vary from state to state, you'll need to ask your local agency what the licensing requirements and standards are for your state. You can also ask your agency if any violations have been reported for centers or homes on your list of prospective settings.

Visiting Child Care Settings

Selecting the type of child care that will work best for your family may take some time. It's important that you visit each child care setting you're considering (seeing a minimum of three is recommended) and, if possible, that you revisit the settings you liked the first time around. While visiting, pay attention to the interactions of the children with each other and with the provider. For a significant portion of any given day, the atmosphere should be pleasant, the children should be engaged in stimulating activities, and the provider should be interacting with or available to the children.

When children are involved, conflicts are inevitable. If a conflict arises while you're visiting, you'll have a wonderful opportunity to see whether the provider responds in a caring and developmentally appropriate way and is sensitive to the children's emotional needs. As they grow and develop, children experience anger and sadness along with all the joys and happiness of childhood. They need the support of knowledgeable, caring adults as they learn to identify and deal with their emotions effectively. In quality child care settings, children receive a lot of adult attention and assistance in learning how to identify and manage their emotions as they participate in activities and interact with other children and adults.

As part of each visit, you'll want to ask the provider or director about her setting's policies and practices. Common policy issues and topics to ask about include injuries and illness, emergencies and disasters, being late, holidays and vacations, bringing toys and other personal belongings from home, television watching, behavior challenges and discipline, toilet training, parent communication and conferences, safety and security, and meals and nutrition. Most homes and centers should have written-down policies. Ask for a copy. If topics you need to know about aren't covered, ask the provider about them and add that information to your copy for future reference.

Quality Child Care Environments

Each child care setting you visit will be different, and the facilities of child care centers will be very different from home care settings. But in any setting, there are general benchmarks of quality care to look for. During a reasonable length of time in a child care setting, you should see these indicators of quality:

1. Children are given the opportunity to engage in large-motor activities, including
- building, sorting, and stacking with a variety of materials such as large blocks;
- organized active small group games and exercises;
- free time to run, jump, and climb both outside and in, in groups and individually.

2. Social interaction is facilitated both formally in small group activities and informally in play with another child or with several other children.

3. Children are given opportunities to develop emerging

literacy, math, science, and artistic skills through age-appropriate play and manipulation of materials of a variety of sizes, shapes, and colors:

- interesting objects to count and sort
- blocks and puzzles for learning spatial relationships
- markers, crayons, and pencils for writing and drawing
- books to read and to have read to them
- building materials that promote problem solving and emerging math skills
- games that involve matching, sequencing, and classification, which are the cornerstones for math and reading

4. Children's creativity is encouraged through opportunities to engage in painting, drawing, singing, dancing, storytelling, and playing with puppets, dolls, and toy animals.

5. The environment is clean and safe for all the children because

- children are supervised at all times by an adult (a minimum adult-to-child ratio of one to four for infants and one to ten for preschool ages is recommended);
- the toys are appropriate for the age of the children and are in good condition;
- there are no safety hazards such as stairs without proper railings, exposed wiring, uncovered outlets, access to tools or medicine, or dangerous pets;
- infants and toddlers are protected from the rough play of older children;

- the atmosphere is pleasant and inviting to children and their families;
- the setting is usually calm and often is filled with the happy sounds of children playing;
- the provider speaks to the children respectfully and maintains discipline without shouting or threatening;
- the children have a secure place where they can keep their personal belongings.

Accreditation

Accreditation is the status given to early childhood programs that have completed an extensive evaluation process based on state and national standards for quality care. To become accredited, a program must participate in an extensive self-study that includes parent evaluation and observation by a trained validation expert. Both child care centers and family child programs may be accredited. Accreditation, however, is not a guarantee of quality. It is a voluntary system to set professional standards and to help families identify high-quality programs. It is simply one tool for helping families evaluate and choose child care.

Provider Credentials

The most important component of quality child care is the relationship your child has with the care provider. Children who have nurturing, responsive, and stable relationships with caring adults generally grow up to be healthier and more competent than children who don't. Research has shown that relationships are a key component to healthy brain development. While observing a child care setting, be sure to look for indications of the relationships the provider has with individual children as well as her rapport with the group. Some questions you may want to ask the provider include the following:

- What experience do you have in working with children, especially children who have characteristics similar to my child's?

- What is your educational experience? The educational requirements for child care providers vary from state to state. Provider credentials can include the completion of a few specific courses, a two-year or four-year college degree in early childhood development, a child development associate degree, a teaching degree, or even a master's degree. Regardless of the type of education a provider has, she or he should be licensed or certified. Studies have shown that one of the best predictors of quality child care is the amount of ongoing training and education the provider receives.

- [if the child care setting is a center] Who are all the people who would be caring for my child and what are their qualifications?

- How long might my child be with a particular provider or teacher? [In other words, what are the teacher turnover rates and, if the children transition to other providers or teachers as they age, how is that transition conducted?]

- What is your philosophy on the care and education of children and what methods do you use? [In other words, how well does the provider's viewpoint fit your family's values and goals?]

The Parent/Provider Relationship

As stressed in this and the other books in this series, the best child care arrangement is one in which the parents and provider work together to provide the guidance, nurturing, and experiences that foster the child's growth and development. A professional child care provider recognizes the parent as the most important influence on the child's development. Good parenting includes seeking information about your child's behavior, interests, skills, and development from knowledgeable resources such as a professional provider. The best way to ensure quality child care is to maintain daily, meaningful communication with your chosen child care provider and to become actively involved in parent activities. Whether you choose a family child care, a child care center, or a professional to care for your child in your home, a quality child care experience should promote your child's health, growth, and education in a fun and safe setting.

Resources for Finding Quality Child Care

www.childcareaware.org (800-424-2246)
A national organization to assist families with child care. This site includes a tool to search for family and center child care in your area. Offered in both English and Spanish.

www.naeyc.org
The National Association for the Education of Young Children. This site has information on accreditation for families as well as a search function for accredited child care centers and kindergartens in your area.

www.nafcc.org
The National Association for Family Child Care. This
site has a search function for accredited family child care
in your area.

About the Authors

Sally Moomaw, MEd is the associate director for professional development at the Arlitt Child and Family Research and Education Center and a clinical faculty member at the University of Cincinnati. She taught preschool and kindergarten children in inclusive classrooms at the Arlitt Center for twenty-two years. Sally is the author or coauthor of nine books, including *Lessons from Turtle Island: Native Curriculum in Early Childhood Programs,* which won the Gustavus Meyers Outstanding Book Award for the study of bigotry and human rights.

Brenda Hieronymus, MEd, is an early childhood education specialist and adjunct instructor at the Arlitt Center, where she teaches young children from diverse cultural and socioeconomic backgrounds, develops and implements state-of-the-art curriculum materials, mentors practicum students, and teaches college courses. She was named Teacher of the Year in 1999 by the Ohio Association for the Education of Young Children.

For over thirty years, Redleaf Press has been a leading publisher of exceptional professional resources for the early childhood field. Redleaf Guides for Parents offer parents field-tested, cutting-edge thinking about creating positive partnerships with the adults who care for their children.